Book of
Revelation

DR. SHARON FORDE-ATIKOSSIE

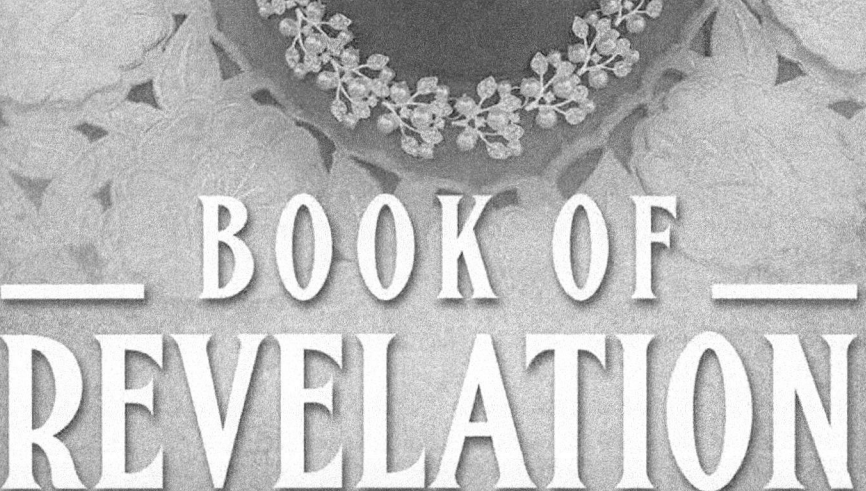

BOOK OF
REVELATION

A SNEAK PEEK ACCORDING TO THE APOSTLE JOHN THE BELOVED

CITI OF BOOKS

CITIOFBOOKS, INC.
3736 Eubank NE Suite A1
Albuquerque, NM 87111-3579
www.citiofbooks.com
Hotline: 1 (877) 389-2759
Fax: 1 (505) 930-7244

Ordering Information:

Quantity sales. Special discounts are available on quantity purchases by corporations, associations, and others. For details, contact the publisher at the address above.

Printed in the United States of America.

ISBN-13:   Softcover   979-8-89391-692-8
                    eBook   979-8-89391-693-5

Library of Congress Control Number: 2025909835

Table of Contents

This is a little preview about the book of revelation prior to your in depth studying that you will be doing in order to get the full impact of what is to come!

It will put your mind at ease, as you look forward to "the rest of the story" as one would say.

Before diving into the content, let us look at the person who wrote this book.

John the Apostle, also known as "The Beloved." He was one of the twelve men who were selected to be an Apostle

He was one of the Twelve Apostles of Jesus according to the New Testament; he was the son of Zebedee and Salome; was Born in Bethsaida; died in 99 AD and was buried in the Basilica of Saint John.

John was known to be the youngest apostle. He was the only apostle that live the longest, and the only apostle that was not killed. He was one of the three that Jesus took to the mountain, and he was one of the people that was at the cross of Jesus.

He was a beloved disciple privileged to rest his head on the Lord's chest, during the Last Supper; he was a fisherman in Galilee until Jesus called him to follow him, and since then John's life was forever transformed.

Of the 12 apostles, John had the privilege of witnessing many of Jesus's miracles, such as giving sight to the blind, and raising the dead.

He was a witness to Jesus crucifixion, and resurrection. He ran to the empty tomb, and saw the resurrected Jesus full of glory and power.

This event reaffirmed John's faith, and mission, and after Jesus ascension he preached the gospel, and cared for the church.

John the Apostle wrote the Book of Revelation, which is the last book in the Holy Bible.

It was written to tell everyone about the future, which is mostly written in symbolic language, using words; pictures, and images.

He expresses that if one thinks that the Book of Revelation is about destruction evil or Satan, people are completely mistaken.

ABOUT THE BOOK

The Book of Revelation tells us, what will happen before, during, and after this event the second coming of Jesus Christ; and the event has predicted three hundred and eighteen times (318) in the Bible making it the most mentioned prediction.

It is a book of great importance, it is vital for the church because as it is written in the book that "blessed is the one who reads aloud the words of this prophecy, and blessed are those who hear it, and take to heart what is written in it because the time is near."

Not forgetting, this is the only book in the Bible that promises a blessing to those who read and hear it.

Studying revelation is crucial because it contains all the prophecies about the end times; prophecies that have not yet been fulfilled but, we believe they will soon be.

Moreover, it is an extremely relevant book for our times, and many believe the end times are approaching and the events of the Book of Revelation will unfold.

Therefore, it is vital that believers read the Book of Revelation to know what is coming and how to be prepared.

DIVING IN
THE BOOK OF REVELATION

John lived in Ephesus where he wrote his gospel in three epistles, exhorting the church to live in God's love and keep the truth; but then came the rise of the fearsome emperor called Domitian, and a very dark time began.

Emperor Domitian was a cruel man who demanded to be worshipped as a God. He demanded an act of loyalty, that went against the very essence of the Christian faith.

Once a year, on the day of the Lord everyone had to burn incense before an altar, and proclaim Caesar is Lord.

For Christians whose devotion was firmly anchored in the declaration of Jesus is Lord, this mandate was a severe challenge. They could not, or must not compromise their faith without facing terrible consequences.

The followers of Christ suffered brutal persecution for proclaiming the gospel, and keeping their testimony firm, and John was sentenced to a horrendous death, where his persecutors with ruthless cruelty condemned him to die in a cauldron of boiling oil.

The intention was clear; a spectacle of death to dissuade others from following Christ, but what happened defied all human logic and showed the miraculous power of God.

The cauldron which was supposed to be John's tomb had no power over him; submerging in the boiling oil he suffered no harm, for the oil which was supposed to consume his flesh became a testimony to divine protection.

His enemies astonished and terrified had no choice but to acknowledge that something supernatural had occurred.

Unable to kill him, they decided to exile him, so they sent him to the island of Patmos, a desolate, and cruel place, where the Roman Empire exiled its enemies to die slowly, it was an island barely 12 kilometers long and six wide which was a rocky wasteland, without streams, trees, or fertile land.

Its aridity, and isolation made it a natural prison, a place where the condemned faced a slow agony, and here John was sent to this inhospitable island.

In exile, this was supposed to be his death sentence, but in the solitude, and suffering of Patmos, he found God's presence in a way he had never experienced before.

In the midst of the rocks, and winds surrounded by the endless sea, the final destiny of humanity and God's eternal glory was revealed to him.

Patmos which was supposed to be John's place of death became the stage for a heavenly vision where he received, and wrote the Book of Revelation.

Therefore the Book of Revelation is a guide, a beacon for those willing to die for what they believed.

Initially, the word martyr simply meant witness, but it soon became clear that being a true witness of Jesus could mean losing one life.

This is why the meaning of martyr changed to someone who dies for their faith Jesus.

The brutality of the Roman persecutions was at its peak, and believers needed a guide; a beacon of hope, and strength in the midst of the darkness.

John begin to delve into his visions that culminated in the Book of Revelation, its symbolism, and the true message behind these texts.

It was the Lord's day, the first day of the week when John was in prayer, but in the midst of his devotion and meditation he felt a profound peace that only the divine presence can bring as his mind was elevated in communion with God, he was caught up in the spirit.

The environment of Patmos faded away, then he found himself in a heavenly realm where reality was more vivid than anything he had experienced on earth.

Suddenly he heard a powerful voice behind him like the sound of a trumpet saying "I am the alpha and the Omega the first, and the last"

The voice resonated with an authority, and majesty that surpassed any earthly sound.

It was a voice John knew the voice of his Lord, Jesus Christ.

`John's heart pounded as he tried to comprehend what was happening, and as he turned to see who was speaking to him and as he did, he saw someone like the son of man who was dressed in a long robe that reached his feet, and was girded with a golden sash around his chest.

His hair was white like wool, like snow, and his eyes were like flames of fire; his feet shone like polished bronze in a furnace and his voice was like the roar of many waters.

Seeing Christ glorified, John understood that he was in the presence of the full manifestation of God.

In his right hand, he held seven stars, and from his mouth came a sharp two edged sword.

The seven stars in his hand represent the angels of the seven churches, and the sharp two edged sword that comes from his mouth symbolizes the word of God; powerful, and penetrating.

John felt as if he was dead, because no one can stand before the holiness of God without being overwhelmed but Christ's hand that came upon him was an act of grace, and comfort assuring John that he is the victor over death and hades.

His face was like the sun shining in its strength.

When John saw him, he fell at his feet as though dead, then he placed his right hand on John and said "do not be afraid I am the first and the last I am the living one; I was dead and now look I am alive forever and ever and I hold the keys of death in <u>Hades</u>".

<u>W</u>hile John lay prostrate before the glorious presence of the son of man, His voice gave John a clear and compelling command "write on a scroll what you see, and to send it to the seven churches to Ephesus Smyrna, Pergamum, Thyatira, Sardis Philadelphia and Leodusea".

John's heart pounded, aware of the magnitude of the task that was entrusted to him.

Every word every vision that would be revealed to him, had to be written with precision, and faithfulness , and John's mission was crucial to convey the divine message to the churches ensuring they understood God's will amidst persecution and trials.

Thus the Book of Revelation was given to John in a unique way no other book in the Bible emerged in such a complex and divine manner.

God the father gave it to Jesus then Jesus gave it to an Angel, and that Angel in turn passed it to John, and he, John wrote it for all the churches.

During his visions, John was taken to heaven where he heard various voices, and choirs singing.

He had to make sure to record all these things accurately. The supernatural nature of his visions was such that he often found himself in a state of awe, and needing the constant guidance of the Angel to stay focused on his task.

John wrote what he saw, and heard, and sometimes what he saw was so extraordinary that the Angel had to remind him up to eleven times, to write it all down.

Every detail was important, and significant. His first visions were actually letters to the seven churches, and so he transmitted them. "To the angel of the church in Symra, write down not to be afraid of what you are about to suffer, I tell you the devil will put some of you in prison to test you, and you will suffer persecution for 10 days. Be faithful even to the point of death, and I will give you life as your victor's crown".

"To the Angel of the church in Pergamum, right I know where you live where Satan has his throne yet you remain true to my name; nevertheless I have a few things against you; there are some among you who hold to the teaching of Balaam repent therefore otherwise I will soon come to you and will fight against them with the sword of my mouth".

"To the Angel of the church in Thyatira, John wrote 'I know your deeds, your love and faith your service , and perseverance. Nevertheless I have this against you. You tolerate that woman Jezebel who calls herself a prophet by her teaching she this leads my servants into sexual immorality and the eating of food sacrificed to idols to the one who is victorious and does my will to the end I will give authority over the nations".

"To the Angel of the church in Sardis, write I know your deeds you have a reputation of being alive, but you are dead wake up strengthen what remains, and is about to die but if you do not wake up I will come like a thief, and you will not know at what time I will come to you".

"To the Angel of the church in Philadelphia, John wrote "See I have placed before you an open door that no one can shut. I know that you have little strength yet you have kept my word and have not denied my name since you have kept my command to endure patiently. I will also keep you from the hour of trial that is going to come on the whole world to test the inhabitants of the earth".

"To the Angel of the church in Laodicea, John wrote "I know your deeds that you are neither cold nor hot I wish you were either one or the other so because you are lukewarm neither hot nor cold I'm about to spit you out of my mouth so be earnest, and repent"

These messages to the churches reflect the spiritual and moral realities of the Christian communities, for Christ praises their virtues and denounces their faults, calling them to repentance, and fidelity.

Each letter contains a promise for those who overcome, emphasizing the importance of perseverance to the end, but a few hours later John was once again taken in the spirit.

After this John looked, and there before him was a door standing open in heaven, and the voice he had first heard speaking to him like a trumpet said "come up here and I will show you what must take place after this.

At once John was in the spirit and he saw a throne in heaven with someone seated on the throne, and his appearance was dazzling like Jasper, and Carnelian, and around the throne was a rainbow that looked like an emerald.

This vision of the throne symbolizes the absolute majesty and sovereignty of God.

The Jasper and Carnelian reflect his purity and justice while the rainbow is a symbol of his covenant, and mercy.

Around the throne John saw twenty four Thrones , and seated on them were twenty four elders clothed in white robes, with golden crowns on their heads.

The 24 elders represent the Saints of all ages, the patriarchs, and apostles, and their white garments symbolized the purity granted by God.

The golden crowns indicate the eternal reward for their faithfulness.

From the throne came flashes of lightning rumblings, and peals of Thunder, and before the throne were seven burning lamps which are the seven spirits of God; also before the throne there was a sea of glass like crystal.

In the midst of the throne, and around it were four living creatures full of eyes in front and behind.

These creatures represent the fullness of creation, vigilant and full of knowledge.

The first living creature was like a lion , the second, like an ox , the third had a face like a man, and the fourth was like a flying eagle.

These living creatures praised day and night saying "holy, holy is the Lord God almighty who was and is and is to come."

Whenever the living creatures give glory honor, and thanks to him who sits on the throne, and who lives forever, and ever.

When ever the 24 elders fall down before him who sits on the throne, and worship him who lives forever and ever, they lay their crowns before the throne and say "you are worthy our Lord and God to receive glory and honor and power for you created all things and by your will they were created have their being".

In the right hand of him who sat on the throne John saw a scroll written inside, and on the back sealed with seven seals.

A mighty angel proclaimed in a loud voice who is worthy to open the scroll, and break its seals but no one in heaven or on earth or under the earth could open the scroll or even look inside it.

John wept much because no one was found worthy. The scroll represents God's sovereign decree for the future; sealed until it's time of fulfillment.

Then one of the elders said to John "do not weep, see the lion of the tribe of Judah the root of David has triumphed to open the scroll and its seven seals."

John turned and saw in the midst of the throne, and the four living creatures and in the midst of the elders a lamb standing as though it had been slain with seven horns and seven eyes, which are the seven spirits of God sent out into all the earth.

This lamb is Christ who has triumphed by his redemptive sacrifice.

The lamb went and took the scroll from the right hand of Him who sat on the throne and when he had taken it the four living creatures and the 24 elders fell down before the lamb.

Each one had a harp and golden bowls full of incense which are the prayers of the Saints and they sang a new song saying "you are worthy to take this rule and to open its seals for you were slain, and by your blood you ransomed people for God from every tribe and language, and people and nation and you have made them a Kingdom and priests to our God, and they shall reign on the earth".

Then he heard the voice of many angels around the throne, and the living creatures and the elders, their number were millions of millions saying with a loud voice "worthy is the lamb who was slain to receive power, and wealth and wisdom and strength and honor and glory and praise."

Then I heard every creature in heaven, and on earth, and under the earth, and on the sea, and all that is in them saying "to him who sits on the throne and to the lamb be praise and honor, and glory and power forever and ever"

Then John watched as the lamb opened one of the seals and he heard one of the four living creatures say with a voice like thunder "come" and John looked, and there was a White Horse, its rider held a bow and a crown that was given to him and he came out conquering, and to conquer this rider represents conquest what is nature can be interpreted as both divine justice and oppression.

When he opened, the second seal John heard the second living creature say "come" and out came another horse bright red, its rider was permitted to take peace from the earth so that people should slay one another, and he was given a great sword.

This rider symbolizes war and bloodshed.

When the lamb opened the third seal John heard the third living creature say "come", and John looked, and there before him was a Black Horse. Its rider was holding a pair of scales in his hand then he heard what sounded like a voice among the four living creatures saying "2 lbs of wheat for a day's wages, and 6 lbs of barley for a day's wages, and do not damage the oil and the wine."

This rider represents famine and scarcity with the skills symbolizing the rationing and high cost of basic foodstuffs.

When he opened the 4th seal John heard the voice of the fourth living creature say "come" and John looked, and behold a pale horse its rider's name was Death, and Hades followed him, and they were given power over a fourth of the earth to kill with sword; with famine; with pestilence; and by wild beasts of the earth.

This rider personifies death in its various forms followed by Hades the place of the dead.

When he opened the 5th seal John saw under the altar the souls of those who had been slain for the word of God and for the testimony they had.

They cried out with a loud voice saying "how long sovereign Lord holy and true until you judge and avenge our blood on those who dwell on the earth".

Then each of them was given a white robe and they were told to rest a little while longer, until the number of their fellow servants and brothers who were to be killed as they had been was completed.

John watched as he opened the 6th seal; there was a great earthquake; the sun turned black like sackcloth made of goat hair; the whole moon turned blood red and the stars in the sky fell to earth as figs dropped from a fig tree when shaken by a strong wind.

The heavens receded like a rule being rolled up, and every mountain and island was removed from its place, then the kings of the earth, the princes, the generals, the rich the mighty, and everyone else, both slave, and free hid in caves, and among the rocks of the mountains.

They called to the mountains, and the rocks "fall on us and hide us from the face of him who sits on the throne and from the wrath of the lamb for the great day of their wrath has come and who can withstand it"

These seals reveal the progressive judgment of God upon the earth the writers symbolize war, conquest, famine and death showing how human sin and rebellion bring destruction.

The martyrs under the altar represent God's justice and his response to the persecution of his people.

The 6th seal with its cataclysms announces the beginning of the final judgment highlighting that creation itself will be convolse before the wrath of God.

Once again John was taken in the spirit to receive visions of future plans, after the 6th seal he saw 4 angels standing at the four corners of the earth holding back the four winds so that no wind would blow on the earth through the sea or any tree.

These angels represent the containment of destruction until God's events are sealed; then John saw another Angel coming up from the east having the seal of the living God.

Then he called out in a loud voice to the four angels who had been given power to harm the land and the sea "do not harm the land or the sea or the trees until we put a seal on the foreheads of the servants of our God, and I heard the number of those sealed; 144,000 from all the tribes of the children of Israel this number,144,000 represents the completeness of the Jewish believers, symbolically whole, and perfect sealed, for divine protection amid judgment.

After this John saw a great multitude that no one could count from every nation tribe, people and language standing before the throne and before the lamb clothed in white robes and holding palm branches in their hands.

They cried out with a loud voice saying "salvation belongs to our God who sits on the throne and to the lamb.

This multitude represents the redeemed gentiles, indicating the universality of the salvation offered by Christ, then one of the elders asked John "these in white robes who are they and where did they come from?" John answered "Sir you know" and he said "these are they who have come out of the great tribulation they have washed their robes and made them white in the blood of the lamb"

Here, the white robes symbolize purity and redemption through Christ's sacrifice. These people have persevered through tribulation, and have received the reward of being in God's presence.

When the lamb opened the 7th seal there was silence in heaven for about half an hour. This solemn silence anticipates the gravity of the judgments to come.

John saw the seven angels who stand before God, and seven trumpets were given to them; another Angel came and stood at the altar holding a golden sensor.

He was given much incense to add to the prayers of all the Saints on the golden altar. Before the throne the smoke of the incense together with the prayers of the Saints went up before God from the angel's hand.

The incense symbolizes the prayers of the Saints showing that our petitions are precious before God and directly before his throne.

The Angel took the sensor filled it with fire from the altar and hurled it to the earth and there were peals of Thunder rumblings flashes of lightning and an earthquake.

The seven angels prepared to sound their trumpets signaling the beginning of catastrophic judgments.

The first Angel sounded his trumpet, and hail and fire mixed with blood were thrown down on the earth.

A third of the earth was burned up; a third of the trees were burned up; and all the green grass was burned up.

This judgment affects the vegetation recalling the plagues of Egypt and demonstrating God's power over nature.

The second Angel sounded his trumpet, and something like a great mountain burning with fire was thrown into the sea; 1/3 of the sea became blood; 1/3 of the living creatures in the sea died, and a third of the ships were destroyed.

This judgment affects the oceans, highlighting large scale devastation.

The third Angel sounded his trumpet, and a great star fell from heaven burning like a torch and it fell on 1/3 of the rivers; and on the springs of water the name of the star is Wormwood; 1/3 of the waters became

Wormwood and many people died from the waters because they had been made bitter.

Here the fresh waters become bitter symbolizing the corruption and contamination of vital sustenance.

The 4th Angel sounded his trumpet, and a third of the sun, 1/3 of the moon, and a third of the stars were struck so that a third of their light was darkened.

1/3 of the day was without light, and also a third of the night. This judgment affects the sources of light, creating chaos and darkness on the earth.

As John watched, he heard an eagle that was flying in midair call out in a loud voice "whoa, whoa, whoa, to the inhabitants of the earth because of the trumpet blasts about to be sounded by the other 3 angels.

This woe announcement indicates that the judgments to come will be even more severe.

The 5th Angel sounded his trumpet and John saw a star that had fallen from the sky to the earth. The star was given the key to the shaft of the abyss, and when he opened the abyss, smoke rose from it like the smoke from a gigantic furnace.

The sun, and sky were darkened by the smoke from the abyss. This fallen star, represents an angelic being possibly Satan with the power to release demonic forces.

Out of the smoke locusts came down upon the earth, and were given power like that of scorpions of the earth they were told not to harm the grass of the earth, or any plant or tree but only those people who did not have the seal of God on their foreheads they were not given power to kill them but only to torture them for five months of the agony they suffered was like that of the sting of a scorpion when it strikes a man.

These demonic locusts symbolize spiritual judgment and internal torment on those who reject God.

The locusts looked like horses prepared for battle, on their heads were something like crowns of gold, their faces resembled human faces, their hair was like women's hair, and their teeth were like lions teeth they had breastplates like breastplates of iron and the sound of their wings was like the thundering of many horses and Chariots rushing into battle.

This description emphasizes their terrifying and destructive nature. They have his king over them the Angel of the abyss whose name in Hebrew is Abaddon, and in Greek, Apollyon Baden, and Apollyon mean destruction and destroyer.

Highlighting the lethal purpose of these demonic forces.

The 6th Angel sounded his trumpet and John heard a voice coming from the four horns of the golden altar that is before God it said to the 6th Angel who had the trumpet "release the four angels who are bound at the great river Euphrates "

These bound angels represent destructive forces that have been restrained until now. The four angels were released to kill 1/3 of mankind.

The number of the mounted troops was 200 million. John heard their number this massive army symbolizes a demonic invasion upon humanity.

The horses and riders, he saw in his vision looked like this' "their breastplates were fiery red dark blue, and yellow as sulfur.

The heads of the horses resembled the heads of lions, and out of their mouths came fire smoke and sulfur 1/3 of mankind was killed by these three plagues ; by the fire ; the smoke; and the sulphur that came out of their mouths.

These plagues symbolized divine judgment, and destruction.

The rest of mankind who were not killed by these plagues still did not repent of the work of their hands; they did not stop worshipping demons, and idols of gold silver bronze stone, and wood. Idols that cannot see or hear or walk; nor did they repent of their murders; their magic arts; their sexual immorality or their thefts.

Despite the judgments many continued in their rebellion showing the hardness of their hearts.

The trumpet judgments reveal the severity of God's judgment and the hardness of the human heart.

The demonic locusts, and the mounted Army underscore the reality of both spiritual, and physical judgment awaiting the ungodly; yet these judgments also serve as a call to repentance a final attempt by God for humanity turn back to him.

Because once again John was taken in the spirit to receive visions of future events. This time John saw another mighty Angel coming down from heaven wrapped in a cloud with a rainbow over his head.

His face was like the sun, and his legs like pillars of fire. This Angel reflects divine majesty, and power with elements symbolizing God's presence.

The Angel had in his hand a little scroll which lay open. He placed his right foot on the sea, and his left foot on the land, and he called out with a loud voice like a lion roaring when he called out, the seven Thunder sounded.

The little scroll symbolizes a specific revelation from God, while the Angel stance indicates his authority over all creation; and when the seven thunders spoke John was about to write but, I heard a voice from heaven say "seal up what the seven thunders have said, and do not write it down."

This command reveals that there are divine mysteries that must not yet be revealed to man. Reminding us of God's sovereignty over knowledge, then Angel, John has seen standing on the sea, and on the land, raised his right hand to heaven, and swore by him who lives forever and ever who created the heavens, and all that is in them.

The earth and all that is in it, and the sea, and all that is in it, that there would be no more delay but, that in the days when the 7th Angel is about to sound this trumpet the mystery of God would be accomplished just as he announced to his servants the prophets, and the voice that I had heard from heaven spoke to me once more "go take the scroll that lies open in the hand of the Angel who is standing on the sea, and on the land,"

So John went to the Angel, and asked him to give me the little scroll he said to him, "take it and eat it; it will turn your stomach sour but in your mouth it will be as sweet as honey"

John took the little scroll from the angel's hand and ate it. It tasted as sweet as honey in his mouth, but when he had eaten it, his stomach turned sour.

This symbolizes, the duality of God's revelation, sweet to receive, but bitter in its fulfillment, and judgment.

Then John was told that he must prophecy again about many people's nations languages and kings.

This reaffirms my mission to proclaim divine truth to all nations.

I was given a read like a measuring rod and was told go and measure the temple of God and the altar with its worshippers but exclude the outer court.

"Do not measure it, because it has been given to the gentiles; They will trample on the holy city for 42 months.

This act of measuring symbolizes the protection and preservation of the faithful while the gentiles represent the persecution of God's people "and I will appoint my two witnesses, and they will prophecy for 1260 days clothed in sackcloth.

These witnesses are the two olive trees and the two lamp stands and they stand before the Lord of the earth

The two witnesses symbolized the constant presence of God's testimony on earth representing the law and the prophets or the church in its prophetic mission.

If anyone tries to harm them fire comes from their mouths and devours their enemies this is how if any anyone who wants to harm them must die.

They have power to shut up the sky so that it will not rain during the time they are prophesying and they have power to turn the waters into blood ,and to strike the earth with every kind of plague as often as they want.

These powers recall Moses and Elijah highlighting the devine authority given to these witnesses.

When they have finished their testimony the beast that comes up from the abyss will attack them and overpower and kill them.

Their bodies will lie in the public square of the great city which is figuratively called Sodom and Egypt where also their Lord was crucified but after 3 1/2 days the breath of life from God entered them, and they stood on their feet and terror struck those who saw them

The 7th Angel sounded his trumpet and there were loud voices in heaven which said "The Kingdom of the world has become the Kingdom of our Lord and of his Messiah and he will reign forever and ever" and the 24 elders who were seated on their Thrones before

God fell on their faces and worshipped God saying "we give thanks to you Lord God almighty the one who is and who was because you have taken your great power and have begun to reign" then God's temple in heaven was opened, and within his temple was seen the ark of his covenant, and there came flashes of lightning rumblings peals of Thunder and earthquake and a severe hail storm this symbolizes God's direct presence in eternal covenant with his people culminating in a complete and final judgment, and a great sign appeared in heaven a woman clothed with the sun with the moon under her feet and a crown of 12 stars on her head she was pregnant and cried out in pain as she was about to give birth.

This woman symbolizes God's people both Israel and the church bringing forth the Messiah into the world.

Another sign appeared in heaven an enormous red dragon with 7 heads and 10 horns and seven crowns on its heads.

I its tail swept 1/3 of the stars out of the sky and flung them to the earth this dragon represents Satan with his power and dominion over earthly kingdoms and his rebellion against God.

The dragon stood in front of the woman who was about to give birth so that it might devour her child the moment he was born. She gave birth to a son a male child who will rule all the nations with an iron scepter and her child was snatched up to God and to his throne the male child is Jesus who is pursued from birth by the forces of evil, but is exalted to heavenly glory.

There was a great battle in heaven Michael and his angels fought against the dragon and the dragon and his angels fought back but, he was not strong enough and they lost their place in heaven the great dragon was hurled down that ancient serpent called the devil or Satan, who leads the whole world astray.

He was hurled to the earth, and his angels with him this war symbolizes satan's defeat and expulsion from heaven reaffirming gods and his angels victory.

Then I heard a loud voice in heaven say "now have come the salvation and the power and the Kingdom of our God and the authority of his Messiah for the accuser of our brothers and sisters who accuses them before our God day and night has been hurled down. They triumphed over him by the blood of the lamb, and by the word of their testimony.

They did not love their lives so much to shrink from death. The dragon filled with fury pursued the woman who had given birth to the male child the woman was given the two wings of a great eagle so that she might fly to the place prepared for her in the wilderness where she would be taken care of for a time times and half a time out of the serpents reach.

The woman protected by God symbolizes the divine refuge and provision for his people during times of persecution.

Then from his mouth the serpent spewed water like a river to overtake the woman, and sweep her away with the torrent but the earth helped the woman by opening its mouth and swallowing the river that the dragon had spewed out of his mouth.

This shows satan's efforts to destroy the church and divine intervention to protect his people.

Then the dragon was enraged at the woman and went off to wage war against the rest of her offspring those who keep God's commands and hold fast their testimony about Jesus.

This indicates the ongoing spiritual battle between the forces of evil, and God's faithful.

Chapters 10, 11 and 12 of revelation reveal the ongoing struggle between good, and evil the sovereign authority of God, and his faithfulness to his people.

The mighty Angel and the little scroll remind us of the duality of divine revelation sweet to receive but bitter in its fulfillment.

The two witnesses symbolize the constant presence of God's testimony on earth; the vision of the woman and the dragon represents the spiritual battle divine protection, and christ's ultimate victory.

These visions call us to remain steadfast in faith trust in God's sovereignty, and persevere amid tribulation, knowing that our redemption is near, and our Lord's victory is sure, and eternal.

After all these incredible visions.

John thought he had experienced every possible emotion but, what he saw next, filled him with awe, and fear for he was shown the forces of evil unleashed on the earth and the resistance of the faithful under God's sovereignty.

These visions would become chapters 13,14 and 15 of the Book of Revelation where they revealed the struggle between good and evil.

The faithfulness of the Saints, and God's final judgment, the beast from the sea and the beast from the earth symbolize oppressive political, and religious powers under satan's influence.

The mark of the beast represents loyalty to evil contrasting with God's seal on the faithful let's begin John saw a beast coming out of the sea it had 10 horns and seven heads with 10 crowns on its horns, and on each head a blasphemous name.

The beast he saw resembled a leopard but had feet like those of a bear and a mouth like that of a lion.

The dragon gave the beast his power, and his throne, and great authority. This beast represents an oppressive political power a coalition of kingdoms acting under satan's influence.

One of the heads of the beast seemed to have had a fatal wound but the fatal wound had been healed the whole world was filled with wonder and followed the beast.

People worshipped the dragon because he had given authority to the beast, and they also worshipped the beast, and asked who is like the beast.

Who can wage war against it. This apparent healing symbolizes evil's ability to regain power and continue deceiving humanity.

The beast was given a mouth to utter proud words, and blasphemies and to exercise its authority for 42 months.

It opened its mouth to blaspheme God, and to slander His name, and His dwelling place, and those who live in heaven.

This duration symbolizes a time of great tribulation , and testing for the faithful. He was given power to wage war against God's holy people unto conquer them, and it was given authority over every tribe people language and nation all inhabitants of the earth will worship the beast all whose names have not been written in the lambs book of life; the lamb who was slain from the creation of the world here we see the intense persecution of believers and the apparent temporary victory of evil.

Then John saw a second beast coming out of the earth, it had two horns like a lamb, but it spoke like a dragon.

It exercised all the authority of the first beast on its behalf, and made the earth and its inhabitants worship the first beast whose fatal wound had been healed.

This second beast symbolizes a false prophet ,or religious system that supports and promotes the power of the first oppressive Kingdom, and it performed great signs even causing fire to come down from heaven to the earth in full view of the people.

Because of the signs it was allowed to perform on behalf of the first beast it deceived the inhabitants of the earth.

It ordered them to set up an image in honor of the beast who was wounded by the sword and yet lived. This deception reveals evil's ability to imitate the divine and confuse humanity the second beast was given power to give breath to the image of the first beast so that the image could speak and cause all who refused to worship the image to be killed.

It also forced all people great, and small rich and poor free and slave to receive a mark on their right hands or on their foreheads so that they could not buy or sell unless they had the mark which is the name of the beast or the number of its name the mark symbolizes loyalty, and submission to this evil power contrasting with God's seal on the faithful.

This calls for wisdom let the person who has insight calculate the number of the beast for it is the number of a man that number is 666 this number 666 symbolizes imperfection and humanity in its fallen state in contrast with divine perfection.

Then John looked and there before me was the lamb standing on Mount Zion and with him 144,000 who had his name and his father's name written on their foreheads, and he heard a sound from heaven like the roar of rushing waters and like a loud peal of Thunder the sound he heard, was like that of harpists playing their harps and they sang a new song before the throne and before the four living creatures, and the elders no one could learn the song except the 144,000 who had been redeemed from the earth. This vision represents the faithful who have persevered and been redeemed marked with loyalty to God.

These are those who did not defile themselves with women, for they remained virgins; they follow the lamb wherever he goes; they were purchased from among mankind and offered his first fruits to God and the lamb no lie was found in their mouths they are blameless the purity and faithfulness of these Saints symbolized true devotion and the holiness required to be in God's presence.

Then John saw another Angel flying in midair and he had the eternal gospel to proclaim to those who live on the earth to every nation tribe language, and people he said in a loud voice "fear God and give him glory" because the hour of his judgment is come worship him who made the heavens the earth the sea, and the springs of water.

This first Angel proclaims the eternal gospel calling humanity to repentance and worship of the true God.

A second Angel followed and said fallen fallen, which is Babylon the great which made all the nations drink the maddening wine of her adulteries.

This second Angel announces the fall of Babylon symbolizing the corruption and moral decay that opposes God.

A third Angel followed them and said in a loud voice "if anyone worships the beast in its image and receives its mark on their forehead or on their hand they too will drink the wine of God's fury which has been poured full strength into the cup of his wrath.

They will be tormented with burning sulfur in the presence of the holy angels, and of the lamb and the smoke of their torment will rise forever, and ever.

There will be no rest day or night for those who worship the beast in its image or for anyone who receives the mark of its name.

This third Angel warns of the fate of those who choose to follow the beast facing God's eternal wrath.

This calls for patient endurance on the part of the people of God who keep his commands, and remain faithful to Jesus.

Then I heard a voice from heaven say "write this, blessed are the dead who die in the Lord from now on.

"Yes" says the spirit, they will rest from their labor for their deeds will follow them. This exhortation is a call to perseverance, and faithfulness, ensuring eternal blessing for those who remain steadfast in their faith.

John looked, and there before him was a white cloud, and seated on the cloud was one like a son of man with a crown of gold on his head, and a sharp sickle in his hand.

Then another Angel came out of the temple, and called in a loud voice to him who was sitting on the cloud, "take your sickle and reap, because the time to reap has come for the harvest of the earth is ripe."

This vision of the harvest symbolizes the final judgment where Christ will separate the righteous from the wicked; so he who was seated on the cloud swung his sickle over the earth, and the earth was harvested.

Another Angel came out of the temple in heaven and he too had a sharp sickle still another Angel who had charge of the fire came from the altar, and called in a loud voice to him "who had the sharp sickle take your sharp sickle and gather the clusters of grapes from the earth's vine because its grapes are ripe.

The Angel swung his sickle on the earth gathered its grapes and threw them into the great wine Press of God's wrath.

This act of gathering symbolizes the collection of the wicked for judgment and God's wrath.

They were trampled in the wine press outside the city, and blood flowed out of the press rising as high as the horses bridles for a distance of 1600 stadia.

This graphic image represents the magnitude of the judgment, and divine retribution on the wicked.

John saw in heaven another great and marvelous sign. 7 angels with the seven last plagues last because with them God's wrath is completed.

These angels represent the final and complete judgment of God on the earth and John saw what looked like a sea of glass glowing, with fire; and standing beside the sea those who had been victorious over the beast and its image and over the number of its name.

They held harps given them by God and sang the song of God's servant Moses and of the lamb "great and marvelous are your deeds Lord God almighty just and true are your ways king of the nations who will not fear you Lord and bring glory to your name for you alone are holy all nations will come and worship before you for your righteous acts have been revealed.

This song celebrates God's justice and holiness, acknowledging his sovereignty over all nations.

After this John looked and he saw in heaven the temple that is the Tabernacle of the covenant law, and it was opened.

Out of the temple, came the seven angels with the seven plagues. They were dressed in clean shining linen, and wore golden sashes around their chests.

These angels dressed in purity authority symbolized the divine execution of final judgment.

Then one of the four living creatures gave to the seven angels 7 golden bowls filled with the wrath of God who lives forever, and ever; and the temple was filled with smoke from the glory of God, and from his power, and no one could under the temple until the seven plagues of the seven angels were completed.

The golden bowls represent the complete wrath of God, and the smoke of his glory symbolizes his supreme holiness, and power.

The visions continue to unfold before John, showing the culmination of divine judgment upon the earth.

John saw the seven angels with the seven bowls of God's wrath prepared to pour out their contents on the world.

The first Angel went and poured out his bowl on the land, and ugly festering sores broke out on the people who had the mark of the beast, and worshipped its image.

These sores symbolized the physical pain and affliction resulting from divine judgment on the followers of the beast.

The second Angel poured out his bowl on the sea, and it turned into blood like that of a dead person, and every living thing in the sea died.

This judgment recalls the plagues of Egypt, showing the death and destruction of marine life symbolizing total judgment on creation.

The third Angel poured out his bowl on the rivers, and springs of water, and they became blood.

Then John heard the Angel in charge of the waters say "you are just in these judgments O holy one, you who are, and who were, for they have shed the blood of your holy people, and your prophets, and you, have given them blood to drink, as they deserve."

This judgment symbolizes divine retribution for the bloodshed of the righteous being.

The fourth angel poured out his bowl on the sun, and the un was allowed to scorch people with fire.

They were seared by the intense and they curse the name of God who had control over these plagues, but they refused to repent, and glorify him.

This judgement symbolizes torment and the hardness of the human heart persisting in rebellion against God.

The 5th Angel poured out his bowl on the throne of the beast and its Kingdom was plunged Into Darkness.

People gnawed their tongues in agony.

This judgment symbolizes confusion and suffering.

In the center of evil power showing the beasts impotence before God's power.

The 6th Angel poured out his bowl on the great river Euphrates and its water was dried up to prepare the way for the kings from the east.

This symbolizes the preparation for the final battle allowing the passage of armies towards their place of destruction.

Then John saw three impure spirits that looked like frogs; they came out of the mouth of the dragon; out of the mouth of the beast; and out of the mouth of the false prophet.

They are demonic spirits that perform signs and they go out to the kings of the whole world to gather them for the battle on the great day of God almighty.

These spirits symbolize the deceptive propaganda of demons leading nations to the final war.

They gathered the kings together to the place that in Hebrew is called Armageddon.

This place symbolizes the ultimate confrontation between the forces of good and evil.

The 7th Angel poured out his bowl into the air and out of the temple came a loud voice from the throne saying "it is done.

Then there came flashes of lightning rumblings peels of Thunder; and a severe earthquake. No earthquake like it has ever occurred.

Since mankind has been on earth so tremendous the quake.

This earthquake symbolizes God's final and total judgment.

The great city split into three parts, and the cities of the nations collapsed.

God remembered Babylon the great, and gave her the cup filled with the wine.

Of the fury of his wrath, Babylon symbolizes the culmination of all evil, and human corruption. Every island fled away, and the mountains could not be found.

From the sky, huge hailstones, each weighing about 100 lbs, fell on people, and they cursed God on account of the plague of hail, because the plague was so terrible.

This hailstorm symbolizes the intensity of the final judgment, and humanities persistent rebellion.

One of the seven angels who had the seven bowls, came and said to John "come I will show you the punishment of the great prostitute who sits by many waters."

The great prostitute symbolizes the corruption, and false religion that seduces nations.

Then the Angel carried John away in the spirit into a wilderness.

There he saw a woman sitting on a scarlet beast that was covered with blasphemous names, and had seven heads and 10 horns.

The woman was dressed in purple, and scarlet, and was glittering with gold; precious stones; and pearls.

She held a golden cup in her hand filled with abominable things, and the filth of her adulteries.

The name written on her forehead was a mystery Babylon.

The great, the mother of prostitutes, and of the abominations of the earth.

The woman and the beast symbolized the alliance between corrupt religion, and evil political power.

John saw that the woman was drunk with the blood of God's Holy people.

The blood of those who bore testimony to Jesus.

When John saw her, he was greatly astonished. Then the Angel said to him, "why are you astonished, I will explain to you the mystery of the woman, and of the beast she rides which has the seven heads and 10 horns.

The beast which you saw once was now, is not and yet will come up out of the abyss, and go to its destruction.

The inhabitants of the earth whose names have not been written in the book of life.

From the creation of the world will be astonished when they see the beast because it once was now, is not and, yet will come.

This symbolizes the apparent resurrection of evil power, and its eventual destruction.

The seven heads are seven hills on which the woman sits.

There are also 7 kings, 5 have fallen; one is the other has not yet come, but when he does come he must remain for only a little while the beast who once was , and now is not is an eighth king.

It belongs to the seven, and is going to his destruction. These heads represent kingdoms, and rulers supporting corruption.

The 10 horns you saw are 10 kings who have not yet received a Kingdom but who for one hour will receive authority, as kings along with the beast they have one purpose, and will give their power, and authority. To the beast, these horns symbolize temporary political alliances with evil power.

They will wage war against the lamb but the lamb will triumph over them, because he is Lord of Lords, and king of kings, and with him, will be his called, chosen, and faithful followers.

This declaration reaffirms Christ, and his followers final victory over evil forces the waters you saw, where the prostitute sits are peoples multitudes nations and languages the beast and the 10 horns you saw, will hate the prostitute. They will bring her to ruin, and leave her naked.

They will eat her flesh and burn her with fire. This final betrayal symbolizes the self destruction of evil.

For God has put it into their hearts to accomplish his purpose by agreeing to hand over to the beast.

Their royal authority until God's words are fulfilled the woman you saw is the great city that rules over the kings of the earth the great city symbolizes the center of corruption and evil power after this I saw another Angel coming down from heaven.

He had great authority and the earth was illuminated by his splendor with a mighty voice he shouted "fallen fallen is Babylon the great she has become a dwelling for demons and a haunt for every impure spirit; a haunt for every unclean bird; a haunt for every unclean and detestable animal.

The fall of Babylon symbolizes the complete and final judgment on all corruption and evil.

John heard another voice from heaven say "come out of her my people so that you will not share in her sins, so that you will not receive any of her plagues.

This call is a warning for believers to separate themselves from evil, and avoid its judgment for her sins are piled up to heaven, and God has remembered her crimes give back to her as she is given.

Pay her back double for what she has done for her a double portion from her own cup give her as much torment, and grief as the glory and luxury she gave herself.

In her heart she boasts "I sit enthroned as queen I am not a widow I will never mourn.

The judgment of Babylon is proportional to her arrogance, and wickedness.

Therefore in one day her plagues will overtake her death.

Mourning and famine she will be consumed by fire for mighty is the Lord God who judges her.

The kings of the earth who committed adultery with her, and shared her luxury.

See the smoke of her burning, they will weep and mourn over her.

Terrified at her torment, they will stand far often cry woe, woe, to you great city, you mighty city of Babylon, and one hour your doom has come.

The lament of kings, and merchants shows the sudden and total destruction of corrupt power, and influence. Another voice from heaven was heard saying "rejoice over her, you heavens rejoice, you people of God rejoice.

Apostles and prophets for God has judged her with the judgment she imposed on you.

This cry of joy in heaven symbolizes the vindication of the Saints and the fulfillment of divine justice.

Then a mighty Angel picked up a boulder the size of a large millstone, and threw it into the sea, and said with such violence the great city of Babylon will be thrown down.

Never to be found again, this symbolizes the irrevocable destruction of Babylon, and the definitive end of its evil influence; and then came the final vision where John witnessed.

The glorious culmination of God's plan.

The scene changed, and John saw heaven open. What he saw filled his heart with hope, and joy; for it was the vision of the ultimate triumph of our Lord Jesus Christ.

After this, he heard what sounded like the roar of a great multitude in heaven shouting "Hallelujah, salvation and, glory, and power belonged to our God for true and just are his judgments.

He has condemned the great prostitute who corrupted the earth by her adulteries.

He has avenged on her the blood of his servants.

The whole heaven united in praise proclaiming the justice, and truth of God's judgments, and again they shouted "Hallelujah."

The smoke from her goes up forever, and ever.

The 24 elders, and the four living creatures, fell down, and worshipped God who was seated on the throne; and they cried" Amen, Hallelujah" then a voice came from the throne saying "praise our God all you his servants, you who fear him both great, and small.

Then John heard what sounded like a great multitude like the roar of rushing waters, and like loud peals of Thunder shouting "Hallelujah for our Lord God almighty reigns, let us rejoice, and be glad, and give him glory for the wedding of the lamb has come, and his bride has made herself ready.

This celebration represents the eternal union of Christ with his church; a relationship of eternal love, and faithfulness.

Then I saw heaven open and behold a White Horse; the one riding it is called faithful and true and in righteousness he judges, and makes war.

His eyes are like a flame of fire, and on his head are many diadems. He has a name written that no one knows but, himself. He is clothed in a robe dipped in blood, and his name is the word of God. This writer is Jesus Christ, the word of God coming in power, and glory to judge, and conquer.

The armies of heaven dressed in fine linen white, and clean followed him on white horses.

From his mouth comes a sharp sword with which to strike down the nations, and he will rule them with a rod of iron. He treads the wine Press of the fury of the wrath of God almighty. The armies represent the Saints, and angels who accompany Christ in his final victory over evil.

John saw the beast, and the kings of the earth and their armies gathered to wage war against the rider on the horse and his army but the beast was captured, and with it the false prophet who had performed the signs on its behalf with these signs he had deluded those who had received the mark of the beast, and worshipped its image.

The two of them were thrown alive into the fiery lake of burning sulfur. The rest were killed with the sword coming out of the mouth of the rider on the horse, and all the birds gorged themselves on their flesh.

This scene shows the final destruction of evil power ensuring that God's justice will prevail. Then John saw an Angel coming down from heaven holding in his hand the key to the abyss, and the great chain he sees the dragon that ancient serpent who is the devil or Satan; and bound him for 1000 years.

He threw him into the abyss and locked, and sealed it over him to keep him from deceiving the nations anymore until the 1000 years were ended. After that he must be set free for a short time; this binding symbolizes the restriction of satan's power preventing him from deceiving the nations. During Christ's millennial reign, John saw Thrones on which were seated.

Those who had been given authority to judge, and he saw the souls of those who had been beheaded because of their testimony about Jesus; and because of the Word of God, they had not worshipped the beast, or its image, and had not received its mark on their foreheads, or their hands.

They came to life, and remained with Christ 1000 years.

These martyrs, and faithful participate in Christ, millennial reign.

An era of peace and justice. The rest of the dead did not come to life until the 1000 years were ended.

This is the first resurrection blessed and holy are those who share in the first resurrection.

The second death has no power over them, but they will be priests of God, and of Christ, and will reign with him for 1000 years.

The first resurrection is the resurrection of the righteous who participate in Christ's reign, and are free from eternal judgment.

When the 1000 years are over. Satan will be released from his prison and will go out to deceive the nations in the four corners of the earth gog and magog and to gather them for battle.

In number they are like the sand on the seashore. They marched across the breadth of the earth, and surrounded the camp of God's people the city he loves but fire came down from heaven, and devoured them.

This temporary release and final defeat of Satan highlight God's complete victory over evil, and the devil who deceived them was thrown into the lake of burning sulfur where the beast, and the false prophet had been thrown.

They will be tormented day, and night forever, and ever. This is the eternal condemnation of Satan, and his followers; then John saw a great white throne in him who was seated on it the earth, and the heavens fled from his presence, and there was no place for them and I saw the dead great and small standing before the throne and books were opened another book was opened which is the book of life; the dead were judged according to what they had done as recorded in the books this final judgment reveals God's perfect justice where every person is judged according to their deeds the sea gave up the dead that were in it, and death, and hades gave up the dead that were in them, and each person was judged according to what they had done. Then death, and hades were thrown into the lake of fire.

The lake of fire is the second death. Anyone whose name was not found written in the book of life, was thrown into the lake of fire.

The second death represents the eternal condemnation for those whose names are not written in the book of life. This vision reveals the culmination of God's plan for humanity's redemption, and judgment.

The second coming of Christ is presented as a glorious, and definitive victory over evil. The lamb is united with his church, and the wedding of the lamb symbolizing the eternal union between Christ and the redeemed.

This revelation forms chapters 19 and 20 of the Book of Revelation. Destruction of the beast, and the false prophet as well as the binding of Satan show the elimination of evil, and the establishment of Christ's Kingdom. The millennial reign symbolizes a period of peace, and justice where the Saints reign with Christ.

The great white throne, judgment is the final manifestation of God's justice where all human beings are judged according to their deeds. Those whose names are written in the book of life are saved, while the wicked face eternal condemnation finally the visions culminated in a glorious, and hope filled revelation.

John saw a new heaven, and a new earth, for the 1st heaven, and the first earth had passed away, and there was no longer any sea.

This new heaven, and new earth symbolized.

The complete renewal of creation free from corruption, and sin, and John saw the holy city, the new Jerusalem coming down out of heaven from God prepared as a bride beautifully dressed for her husband.

This Holy City represents the eternal dwelling place of God with his people adorned with beauty, and holiness prepared as a bride for Christ, and John heard a loud voice from the throne saying "look God's dwelling place is now among the people, and he will dwell with them.

They will be his people, and God himself will be with them, and be their God.

He will wipe every tear from their eyes. There will be no more death, or mourning, or crying, or pain for the old order of things has passed away.

This divine promise assures that suffering, and death will be eliminated, and God himself will live among his people bringing eternal comfort, and peace. He who was seated on the throne said "I am making everything new" then he said "write this down for these words are trustworthy, and true he said to me "it is done I am the alpha, and the Omega the beginning and the end. To the thirsty I will give water without cost from the spring of the water of life those who are victorious, will inherit all this and I will be their God, and they will be my children"

This promise of eternal life, and divine inheritance was reserved for those who persevere in faith, but the cowardly, the unbelieving ; the vile the murderers; the sexually immoral.

Those who practice magic arts; the idolaters; and all liars.

They will be consigned to the fiery lake of burning sulfur.

This is the second death. This final judgment ensures that those who persist in evil are excluded from eternal blessing.

One of the seven angels who had the seven bowls full of the seven last plagues came, and said to me "come I will show you the bride, the wife of the lamb, and he carried John away in the spirit to a mountain great and high; and showed him the holy city Jerusalem coming down out of heaven from God.

It shone with the glory of God, and its brilliance was like that of a very precious jewel like a Jasper, clear as crystal. It had a great high wall with 12 gates, and with 12 angels at the gates on the gates were written.

The names of the 12 tribes of Israel. These gates and foundations represent the fullness of God's people; both from the old, and new covenants.

The Angel who talked with John had a measuring rod of gold to measure the city.

Its gates, and its walls the city was laid out like a square as long as it was wide.

He measured the city with the rod, and found it to be 12,000 stadia in length, and as wide, and high as it is long.

The perfect dimensions of the city symbolize the perfection of God's Kingdom.

The wall was made of Jasper, and the city of pure gold as pure as glass the foundations of the city walls were decorated with every kind of precious stone. The precious materials, and pure gold reflect the purity holiness, and eternal value of the new Jerusalem.

24 hours John did not see a temple in the city because the Lord God almighty, and the lamb are.

Its temple, the city does not need the sun or the moon to shine on it for the glory of God gives it light, and the lamb is its lamp, the presence of God, and the lamb replaces any need for a physical temple was their glory illuminates. Everything the nations will walk by its light, and the kings of the earth will bring their splendor into it on no day will its gates ever be shut for, there will be no night.

There the glory, and honor of the nations will be brought into it. Nothing impure will ever enter it, nor will anyone who does what is shameful, or deceitful; but only those whose names are written in the lambs book of life.

The open gate symbolizes perpetual accessibility, and welcome for the redeemed while the exclusion of the impure ensures the eternal purity of the city.

Then the Angel showed John the river of the water of life as clear as crystal flowing from the throne of God, and of the lamb down the middle of the great St. of the city on each side of the river stood the tree of life bearing 12 crops of fruit yielding its fruit every month, and the leaves of the tree are for the healing of the nations.

This river of life, and the tree of life symbolize the eternal life, and healing flowing from God's presence.

No longer will there be any curse.

The throne of God, and of the lamb will be in the city, and his servants will serve him. They will see his face, and his name will be on their foreheads.

There will be no more night, they will not need the light of a lamp or the light of the sun for the Lord God will give them light, and they will reign forever, and ever.

The absence of the curse, and the presence of God's throne indicate complete restoration, and eternal communion with God.

He said to me, these words are trustworthy, and true.

The Lord, the God who inspires the prophets sent his Angel to show his servants the things that must soon take place "look I am coming soon; blessed is the one who keeps the words of the prophecy" Written in this scroll this confirmation, reaffirms the truth, and urgency of the prophecies revealed. He, John is the one who heard, and saw these things, and when John had heard, and seen them he fell down to worship at the feet of the Angel who had been showing them to him; but he said to John "don't do that, I'm a fellow servant with you, and with your fellow prophets and with all who keep the words of this scroll; worship God." This call to worship, God alone underscores the centrality of true and exclusive worship of the creator.

He told John "do not seal up the words of the prophecy of this scroll because the time is near. Let the one who does wrong; continue to do wrong. Let the vile person continue to be vile. Let the one who Lies, might continue to do right, and let the holy person continue to be holy.

The imminence of these prophecies calls for an urgent decision of holiness, and righteousness.

"look I am coming soon, my reward is with me and I will give to each person according to what they have done I am the alpha and the Omega the 1st and the last; the beginning and the end.

The promise of christ's coming with his reward highlights divine justice in the believers hope. Blessed are those who wash their robes that they may have the right to the tree of life, and may go through the gates into the city.

Outside are the dogs. Those who practice magic arts; the sexually immoral; the murderers the idolaters; and everyone who loves; and practices falsehood; the blessing upon those who wash their robes in the lamb's blood underscores the purity needed to enter the new Jerusalem.

"I Jesus have sent my Angel to give you this testimony for the churches I am the root in the offspring of David and the bright morning star the spirit and the bride say "come and let the one who hears" say "come, let the one who is thirsty come and let the one who wishes take the free gift of the water of life Jesus." Testimony reaffirms his messianic identity, and the open invitation to all to receive eternal life I warn everyone who hears the words of the prophecy of this scroll. If anyone adds anything to them, God will add to that person the plagues described in this scroll, and if anyone takes words away from this scroll of prophecy God will take away from that person.

Any share in the tree of life, and in the holy city which are described in this scroll.

THIS FINAL WARNING

O k there Jesus he affirms his messianic identity, and the open invitation to all to receive eternal life.

John warn everyone who hears the words of the prophecy of this scroll if anyone adds anything to them God will add to that person the plagues described in this scroll, and if anyone takes words away from this scroll of prophecy, God will take away from that person any share in the tree of life and in the holy city which are described on the scroll this final warning, ensures the integrity of the prophetic message who testifies to these things says yes I am coming soon Amen.

"Come Lord Jesus" John's response expresses the longing for the Lord's coming the grace of the Lord Jesus be with God's people Amen.

This final blessing assures Christ grace and continual presence with his people chapters 21 and 22 of the Book of Revelation reveal the glorious culmination of God's plan the creation of a new heaven, and a new earth, and the manifestation of the new Jerusalem.

God's dwelling among his people eliminates all suffering, and death bringing eternal peace, and comfort the holy city symbolizes the purity, and perfection of God's eternal Kingdom.

The river of life and the tree of life represent the eternal life, and healing that flow from God's presence.

The confirmation of prophecy the call to worship, and the promise of Christ coming highlight the urgency, and hope of the message.

These chapters call everyone to live in holiness, and to eagerly await the coming of our Lord Jesus Christ; to remain steadfast in faith knowing that the end of all things is God's victory.

REVELATION CHAPTER 1-22
REVELATION 1-22
KING JAMES VERSION

1 The Revelation of Jesus Christ, which God gave unto him, to shew unto his servants things which must shortly come to pass; and he sent and signified it by his angel unto his servant John:

2 Who bare record of the word of God, and of the testimony of Jesus Christ, and of all things that he saw.

3 Blessed is he that readeth, and they that hear the words of this prophecy, and keep those things which are written therein: for the time is at hand.

4 John to the seven churches which are in Asia: Grace be unto you, and peace, from him which is, and which was, and which is to come; and from the seven Spirits which are before his throne;

5 And from Jesus Christ, who is the faithful witness, and the first begotten of the dead, and the prince of the kings of the earth. Unto him that loved us, and washed us from our sins in his own blood,

6 And hath made us kings and priests unto God and his Father; to him be glory and dominion for ever and ever. Amen.

⁷ Behold, he cometh with clouds; and every eye shall see him, and they also which pierced him: and all kindreds of the earth shall wail because of him. Even so, Amen.

⁸ I am Alpha and Omega, the beginning and the ending, saith the Lord, which is, and which was, and which is to come, the Almighty.

⁹ I John, who also am your brother, and companion in tribulation, and in the kingdom and patience of Jesus Christ, was in the isle that is called Patmos, for the word of God, and for the testimony of Jesus Christ.

¹⁰ I was in the Spirit on the Lord's day, and heard behind me a great voice, as of a trumpet,

¹¹ Saying, I am Alpha and Omega, the first and the last: and, What thou seest, write in a book, and send it unto the seven churches which are in Asia; unto Ephesus, and unto Smyrna, and unto Pergamos, and unto Thyatira, and unto Sardis, and unto Philadelphia, and unto Laodicea.

¹² And I turned to see the voice that spake with me. And being turned, I saw seven golden candlesticks;

¹³ And in the midst of the seven candlesticks one like unto the Son of man, clothed with a garment down to the foot, and girt about the paps with a golden girdle.

¹⁴ His head and his hairs were white like wool, as white as snow; and his eyes were as a flame of fire;

¹⁵ And his feet like unto fine brass, as if they burned in a furnace; and his voice as the sound of many waters.

¹⁶ And he had in his right hand seven stars: and out of his mouth went a sharp twoedged sword: and his countenance was as the sun shineth in his strength.

¹⁷ And when I saw him, I fell at his feet as dead. And he laid his right hand upon me, saying unto me, Fear not; I am the first and the last:

¹⁸ I am he that liveth, and was dead; and, behold, I am alive for evermore, Amen; and have the keys of hell and of death.

¹⁹ Write the things which thou hast seen, and the things which are, and the things which shall be hereafter;

²⁰ The mystery of the seven stars which thou sawest in my right hand, and the seven golden candlesticks. The seven stars are the angels of the seven churches: and the seven candlesticks which thou sawest are the seven churches.

2 Unto the angel of the church of Ephesus write; These things saith he that holdeth the seven stars in his right hand, who walketh in the midst of the seven golden candlesticks;

² I know thy works, and thy labour, and thy patience, and how thou canst not bear them which are evil: and thou hast tried them which say they are apostles, and are not, and hast found them liars:

³ And hast borne, and hast patience, and for my name's sake hast laboured, and hast not fainted.

⁴ Nevertheless I have somewhat against thee, because thou hast left thy first love.

⁵ Remember therefore from whence thou art fallen, and repent, and do the first works; or else I will come unto thee quickly, and will remove thy candlestick out of his place, except thou repent.

⁶ But this thou hast, that thou hatest the deeds of the Nicolaitanes, which I also hate.

⁷ He that hath an ear, let him hear what the Spirit saith unto the churches; To him that overcometh will I give to eat of the tree of life, which is in the midst of the paradise of God.

⁸ And unto the angel of the church in Smyrna write; These things saith the first and the last, which was dead, and is alive;

⁹ I know thy works, and tribulation, and poverty, (but thou art rich) and I know the blasphemy of them which say they are Jews, and are not, but are the synagogue of Satan.

¹⁰ Fear none of those things which thou shalt suffer: behold, the devil shall cast some of you into prison, that ye may be tried; and ye shall have tribulation ten days: be thou faithful unto death, and I will give thee a crown of life.

¹¹ He that hath an ear, let him hear what the Spirit saith unto the churches; He that overcometh shall not be hurt of the second death.

¹² And to the angel of the church in Pergamos write; These things saith he which hath the sharp sword with two edges;

¹³ I know thy works, and where thou dwellest, even where Satan's seat is: and thou holdest fast my name, and hast not denied my faith, even in those days wherein Antipas was my faithful martyr, who was slain among you, where Satan dwelleth.

¹⁴ But I have a few things against thee, because thou hast there them that hold the doctrine of Balaam, who taught Balac to cast a stumblingblock before the children of Israel, to eat things sacrificed unto idols, and to commit fornication.

¹⁵ So hast thou also them that hold the doctrine of the Nicolaitanes, which thing I hate.

¹⁶ Repent; or else I will come unto thee quickly, and will fight against them with the sword of my mouth.

¹⁷ He that hath an ear, let him hear what the Spirit saith unto the churches; To him that overcometh will I give to eat of the hidden manna, and will give him a white stone, and in the stone a new name written, which no man knoweth saving he that receiveth it.

¹⁸ And unto the angel of the church in Thyatira write; These things saith the Son of God, who hath his eyes like unto a flame of fire, and his feet are like fine brass;

¹⁹ I know thy works, and charity, and service, and faith, and thy patience, and thy works; and the last to be more than the first.

²⁰ Notwithstanding I have a few things against thee, because thou sufferest that woman Jezebel, which calleth herself a prophetess, to teach and to seduce

my servants to commit fornication, and to eat things sacrificed unto idols.

²¹ And I gave her space to repent of her fornication; and she repented not.

²² Behold, I will cast her into a bed, and them that commit adultery with her into great tribulation, except they repent of their deeds.

²³ And I will kill her children with death; and all the churches shall know that I am he which searcheth the reins and hearts: and I will give unto every one of you according to your works.

²⁴ But unto you I say, and unto the rest in Thyatira, as many as have not this doctrine, and which have not known the depths of Satan, as they speak; I will put upon you none other burden.

²⁵ But that which ye have already hold fast till I come.

²⁶ And he that overcometh, and keepeth my works unto the end, to him will I give power over the nations:

²⁷ And he shall rule them with a rod of iron; as the vessels of a potter shall they be broken to shivers: even as I received of my Father.

²⁸ And I will give him the morning star.

²⁹ He that hath an ear, let him hear what the Spirit saith unto the churches.

3 And unto the angel of the church in Sardis write; These things saith he that hath the seven Spirits of God, and the seven stars; I know thy works, that thou hast a name that thou livest, and art dead.

² Be watchful, and strengthen the things which remain, that are ready to die: for I have not found thy works perfect before God.

³ Remember therefore how thou hast received and heard, and hold fast, and repent. If therefore thou shalt not watch, I will come on thee as a thief, and thou shalt not know what hour I will come upon thee.

⁴ Thou hast a few names even in Sardis which have not defiled their garments; and they shall walk with me in white: for they are worthy.

⁵ He that overcometh, the same shall be clothed in white raiment; and I will not blot out his name out of the book of life, but I will confess his name before my Father, and before his angels.

⁶ He that hath an ear, let him hear what the Spirit saith unto the churches.

⁷ And to the angel of the church in Philadelphia write; These things saith he that is holy, he that is true, he that hath the key of David, he that openeth, and no man shutteth; and shutteth, and no man openeth;

⁸ I know thy works: behold, I have set before thee an open door, and no man can shut it: for thou hast a little strength, and hast kept my word, and hast not denied my name.

⁹ Behold, I will make them of the synagogue of Satan, which say they are Jews, and are not, but do lie; behold, I will make them to come and worship before thy feet, and to know that I have loved thee.

¹⁰ Because thou hast kept the word of my patience, I also will keep thee from the hour of temptation, which shall come upon all the world, to try them that dwell upon the earth.

¹¹ Behold, I come quickly: hold that fast which thou hast, that no man take thy crown.

¹² Him that overcometh will I make a pillar in the temple of my God, and he shall go no more out: and I will write upon him the name of my God, and the name of the city of my God, which is new Jerusalem, which cometh down out of heaven from my God: and I will write upon him my new name.

¹³ He that hath an ear, let him hear what the Spirit saith unto the churches.

¹⁴ And unto the angel of the church of the Laodiceans write; These things saith the Amen, the faithful and true witness, the beginning of the creation of God;

¹⁵ I know thy works, that thou art neither cold nor hot: I would thou wert cold or hot.

¹⁶ So then because thou art lukewarm, and neither cold nor hot, I will spue thee out of my mouth.

¹⁷ Because thou sayest, I am rich, and increased with goods, and have need of nothing; and knowest not that thou art wretched, and miserable, and poor, and blind, and naked:

¹⁸ I counsel thee to buy of me gold tried in the fire, that thou mayest be rich; and white raiment, that thou mayest be clothed, and that the shame of thy nakedness

do not appear; and anoint thine eyes with eyesalve, that thou mayest see.

¹⁹ As many as I love, I rebuke and chasten: be zealous therefore, and repent.

²⁰ Behold, I stand at the door, and knock: if any man hear my voice, and open the door, I will come in to him, and will sup with him, and he with me.

²¹ To him that overcometh will I grant to sit with me in my throne, even as I also overcame, and am set down with my Father in his throne.

²² He that hath an ear, let him hear what the Spirit saith unto the churches.

4 After this I looked, and, behold, a door was opened in heaven: and the first voice which I heard was as it were of a trumpet talking with me; which said, Come up hither, and I will shew thee things which must be hereafter.

² And immediately I was in the spirit: and, behold, a throne was set in heaven, and one sat on the throne.

³ And he that sat was to look upon like a jasper and a sardine stone: and there was a rainbow round about the throne, in sight like unto an emerald.

⁴ And round about the throne were four and twenty seats: and upon the seats I saw four and twenty elders sitting, clothed in white raiment; and they had on their heads crowns of gold.

⁵ And out of the throne proceeded lightnings and thunderings and voices: and there were seven lamps

of fire burning before the throne, which are the seven Spirits of God.

⁶ And before the throne there was a sea of glass like unto crystal: and in the midst of the throne, and round about the throne, were four beasts full of eyes before and behind.

⁷ And the first beast was like a lion, and the second beast like a calf, and the third beast had a face as a man, and the fourth beast was like a flying eagle.

⁸ And the four beasts had each of them six wings about him; and they were full of eyes within: and they rest not day and night, saying, Holy, holy, holy, Lord God Almighty, which was, and is, and is to come.

⁹ And when those beasts give glory and honour and thanks to him that sat on the throne, who liveth for ever and ever,

¹⁰ The four and twenty elders fall down before him that sat on the throne, and worship him that liveth for ever and ever, and cast their crowns before the throne, saying,

¹¹ Thou art worthy, O Lord, to receive glory and honour and power: for thou hast created all things, and for thy pleasure they are and were created.

5 And I saw in the right hand of him that sat on the throne a book written within and on the backside, sealed with seven seals.

² And I saw a strong angel proclaiming with a loud voice, Who is worthy to open the book, and to loose the seals thereof?

³ And no man in heaven, nor in earth, neither under the earth, was able to open the book, neither to look thereon.

⁴ And I wept much, because no man was found worthy to open and to read the book, neither to look thereon.

⁵ And one of the elders saith unto me, Weep not: behold, the Lion of the tribe of Judah, the Root of David, hath prevailed to open the book, and to loose the seven seals thereof.

⁶ And I beheld, and, lo, in the midst of the throne and of the four beasts, and in the midst of the elders, stood a Lamb as it had been slain, having seven horns and seven eyes, which are the seven Spirits of God sent forth into all the earth.

⁷ And he came and took the book out of the right hand of him that sat upon the throne.

⁸ And when he had taken the book, the four beasts and four and twenty elders fell down before the Lamb, having every one of them harps, and golden vials full of odours, which are the prayers of saints.

⁹ And they sung a new song, saying, Thou art worthy to take the book, and to open the seals thereof: for thou wast slain, and hast redeemed us to God by thy blood out of every kindred, and tongue, and people, and nation;

¹⁰ And hast made us unto our God kings and priests: and we shall reign on the earth.

¹¹ And I beheld, and I heard the voice of many angels round about the throne and the beasts and the elders:

and the number of them was ten thousand times ten thousand, and thousands of thousands;

¹² Saying with a loud voice, Worthy is the Lamb that was slain to receive power, and riches, and wisdom, and strength, and honour, and glory, and blessing.

¹³ And every creature which is in heaven, and on the earth, and under the earth, and such as are in the sea, and all that are in them, heard I saying, Blessing, and honour, and glory, and power, be unto him that sitteth upon the throne, and unto the Lamb for ever and ever.

¹⁴ And the four beasts said, Amen. And the four and twenty elders fell down and worshipped him that liveth for ever and ever.

6 And I saw when the Lamb opened one of the seals, and I heard, as it were the noise of thunder, one of the four beasts saying, Come and see.

² And I saw, and behold a white horse: and he that sat on him had a bow; and a crown was given unto him: and he went forth conquering, and to conquer.

³ And when he had opened the second seal, I heard the second beast say, Come and see.

⁴ And there went out another horse that was red: and power was given to him that sat thereon to take peace from the earth, and that they should kill one another: and there was given unto him a great sword.

⁵ And when he had opened the third seal, I heard the third beast say, Come and see. And I beheld, and lo a black horse; and he that sat on him had a pair of balances in his hand.

⁶ And I heard a voice in the midst of the four beasts say, A measure of wheat for a penny, and three measures of barley for a penny; and see thou hurt not the oil and the wine.

⁷ And when he had opened the fourth seal, I heard the voice of the fourth beast say, Come and see.

⁸ And I looked, and behold a pale horse: and his name that sat on him was Death, and Hell followed with him. And power was given unto them over the fourth part of the earth, to kill with sword, and with hunger, and with death, and with the beasts of the earth.

⁹ And when he had opened the fifth seal, I saw under the altar the souls of them that were slain for the word of God, and for the testimony which they held:

¹⁰ And they cried with a loud voice, saying, How long, O Lord, holy and true, dost thou not judge and avenge our blood on them that dwell on the earth?

¹¹ And white robes were given unto every one of them; and it was said unto them, that they should rest yet for a little season, until their fellowservants also and their brethren, that should be killed as they were, should be fulfilled.

¹² And I beheld when he had opened the sixth seal, and, lo, there was a great earthquake; and the sun became black as sackcloth of hair, and the moon became as blood;

¹³ And the stars of heaven fell unto the earth, even as a fig tree casteth her untimely figs, when she is shaken of a mighty wind.

¹⁴ And the heaven departed as a scroll when it is rolled together; and every mountain and island were moved out of their places.

¹⁵ And the kings of the earth, and the great men, and the rich men, and the chief captains, and the mighty men, and every bondman, and every free man, hid themselves in the dens and in the rocks of the mountains;

¹⁶ And said to the mountains and rocks, Fall on us, and hide us from the face of him that sitteth on the throne, and from the wrath of the Lamb:

¹⁷ For the great day of his wrath is come; and who shall be able to stand?

7 And after these things I saw four angels standing on the four corners of the earth, holding the four winds of the earth, that the wind should not blow on the earth, nor on the sea, nor on any tree.

² And I saw another angel ascending from the east, having the seal of the living God: and he cried with a loud voice to the four angels, to whom it was given to hurt the earth and the sea,

³ Saying, Hurt not the earth, neither the sea, nor the trees, till we have sealed the servants of our God in their foreheads.

⁴ And I heard the number of them which were sealed: and there were sealed an hundred and forty and four thousand of all the tribes of the children of Israel.

⁵ Of the tribe of Juda were sealed twelve thousand. Of the tribe of Reuben were sealed twelve thousand. Of the tribe of Gad were sealed twelve thousand.

⁶ Of the tribe of Aser were sealed twelve thousand. Of the tribe of Nephthalim were sealed twelve thousand. Of the tribe of Manasses were sealed twelve thousand.

⁷ Of the tribe of Simeon were sealed twelve thousand. Of the tribe of Levi were sealed twelve thousand. Of the tribe of Issachar were sealed twelve thousand.

⁸ Of the tribe of Zabulon were sealed twelve thousand. Of the tribe of Joseph were sealed twelve thousand. Of the tribe of Benjamin were sealed twelve thousand.

⁹ After this I beheld, and, lo, a great multitude, which no man could number, of all nations, and kindreds, and people, and tongues, stood before the throne, and before the Lamb, clothed with white robes, and palms in their hands;

¹⁰ And cried with a loud voice, saying, Salvation to our God which sitteth upon the throne, and unto the Lamb.

¹¹ And all the angels stood round about the throne, and about the elders and the four beasts, and fell before the throne on their faces, and worshipped God,

¹² Saying, Amen: Blessing, and glory, and wisdom, and thanksgiving, and honour, and power, and might, be unto our God for ever and ever. Amen.

¹³ And one of the elders answered, saying unto me, What are these which are arrayed in white robes? and whence came they?

¹⁴ And I said unto him, Sir, thou knowest. And he said to me, These are they which came out of great tribulation,

and have washed their robes, and made them white in the blood of the Lamb.

¹⁵ Therefore are they before the throne of God, and serve him day and night in his temple: and he that sitteth on the throne shall dwell among them.

¹⁶ They shall hunger no more, neither thirst any more; neither shall the sun light on them, nor any heat.

¹⁷ For the Lamb which is in the midst of the throne shall feed them, and shall lead them unto living fountains of waters: and God shall wipe away all tears from their eyes.

8 And when he had opened the seventh seal, there was silence in heaven about the space of half an hour.

² And I saw the seven angels which stood before God; and to them were given seven trumpets.

³ And another angel came and stood at the altar, having a golden censer; and there was given unto him much incense, that he should offer it with the prayers of all saints upon the golden altar which was before the throne.

⁴ And the smoke of the incense, which came with the prayers of the saints, ascended up before God out of the angel's hand.

⁵ And the angel took the censer, and filled it with fire of the altar, and cast it into the earth: and there were voices, and thunderings, and lightnings, and an earthquake.

⁶ And the seven angels which had the seven trumpets prepared themselves to sound.

7 The first angel sounded, and there followed hail and fire mingled with blood, and they were cast upon the earth: and the third part of trees was burnt up, and all green grass was burnt up.

8 And the second angel sounded, and as it were a great mountain burning with fire was cast into the sea: and the third part of the sea became blood;

9 And the third part of the creatures which were in the sea, and had life, died; and the third part of the ships were destroyed.

10 And the third angel sounded, and there fell a great star from heaven, burning as it were a lamp, and it fell upon the third part of the rivers, and upon the fountains of waters;

11 And the name of the star is called Wormwood: and the third part of the waters became wormwood; and many men died of the waters, because they were made bitter.

12 And the fourth angel sounded, and the third part of the sun was smitten, and the third part of the moon, and the third part of the stars; so as the third part of them was darkened, and the day shone not for a third part of it, and the night likewise.

13 And I beheld, and heard an angel flying through the midst of heaven, saying with a loud voice, Woe, woe, woe, to the inhabiters of the earth by reason of the other voices of the trumpet of the three angels, which are yet to sound!

9 And the fifth angel sounded, and I saw a star fall from heaven unto the earth: and to him was given the key of the bottomless pit.

² And he opened the bottomless pit; and there arose a smoke out of the pit, as the smoke of a great furnace; and the sun and the air were darkened by reason of the smoke of the pit.

³ And there came out of the smoke locusts upon the earth: and unto them was given power, as the scorpions of the earth have power.

⁴ And it was commanded them that they should not hurt the grass of the earth, neither any green thing, neither any tree; but only those men which have not the seal of God in their foreheads.

⁵ And to them it was given that they should not kill them, but that they should be tormented five months: and their torment was as the torment of a scorpion, when he striketh a man.

⁶ And in those days shall men seek death, and shall not find it; and shall desire to die, and death shall flee from them.

⁷ And the shapes of the locusts were like unto horses prepared unto battle; and on their heads were as it were crowns like gold, and their faces were as the faces of men.

⁸ And they had hair as the hair of women, and their teeth were as the teeth of lions.

⁹ And they had breastplates, as it were breastplates of iron; and the sound of their wings was as the sound of chariots of many horses running to battle.

¹⁰ And they had tails like unto scorpions, and there were stings in their tails: and their power was to hurt men five months.

¹¹ And they had a king over them, which is the angel of the bottomless pit, whose name in the Hebrew tongue is Abaddon, but in the Greek tongue hath his name Apollyon.

¹² One woe is past; and, behold, there come two woes more hereafter.

¹³ And the sixth angel sounded, and I heard a voice from the four horns of the golden altar which is before God,

¹⁴ Saying to the sixth angel which had the trumpet, Loose the four angels which are bound in the great river Euphrates.

¹⁵ And the four angels were loosed, which were prepared for an hour, and a day, and a month, and a year, for to slay the third part of men.

¹⁶ And the number of the army of the horsemen were two hundred thousand thousand: and I heard the number of them.

¹⁷ And thus I saw the horses in the vision, and them that sat on them, having breastplates of fire, and of jacinth, and brimstone: and the heads of the horses were as the heads of lions; and out of their mouths issued fire and smoke and brimstone.

¹⁸ By these three was the third part of men killed, by the fire, and by the smoke, and by the brimstone, which issued out of their mouths.

¹⁹ For their power is in their mouth, and in their tails: for their tails were like unto serpents, and had heads, and with them they do hurt.

²⁰ And the rest of the men which were not killed by these plagues yet repented not of the works of their hands, that they should not worship devils, and idols of gold, and silver, and brass, and stone, and of wood: which neither can see, nor hear, nor walk:

²¹ Neither repented they of their murders, nor of their sorceries, nor of their fornication, nor of their thefts.

10 And I saw another mighty angel come down from heaven, clothed with a cloud: and a rainbow was upon his head, and his face was as it were the sun, and his feet as pillars of fire:

² And he had in his hand a little book open: and he set his right foot upon the sea, and his left foot on the earth,

³ And cried with a loud voice, as when a lion roareth: and when he had cried, seven thunders uttered their voices.

⁴ And when the seven thunders had uttered their voices, I was about to write: and I heard a voice from heaven saying unto me, Seal up those things which the seven thunders uttered, and write them not.

⁵ And the angel which I saw stand upon the sea and upon the earth lifted up his hand to heaven,

⁶ And sware by him that liveth for ever and ever, who created heaven, and the things that therein are, and the earth, and the things that therein are, and the sea, and the things which are therein, that there should be time no longer:

⁷ But in the days of the voice of the seventh angel, when he shall begin to sound, the mystery of God should be finished, as he hath declared to his servants the prophets.

⁸ And the voice which I heard from heaven spake unto me again, and said, Go and take the little book which is open in the hand of the angel which standeth upon the sea and upon the earth.

⁹ And I went unto the angel, and said unto him, Give me the little book. And he said unto me, Take it, and eat it up; and it shall make thy belly bitter, but it shall be in thy mouth sweet as honey.

¹⁰ And I took the little book out of the angel's hand, and ate it up; and it was in my mouth sweet as honey: and as soon as I had eaten it, my belly was bitter.

¹¹ And he said unto me, Thou must prophesy again before many peoples, and nations, and tongues, and kings.

11 And there was given me a reed like unto a rod: and the angel stood, saying, Rise, and measure the temple of God, and the altar, and them that worship therein.

² But the court which is without the temple leave out, and measure it not; for it is given unto the Gentiles:

and the holy city shall they tread under foot forty and two months.

³ And I will give power unto my two witnesses, and they shall prophesy a thousand two hundred and threescore days, clothed in sackcloth.

⁴ These are the two olive trees, and the two candlesticks standing before the God of the earth.

⁵ And if any man will hurt them, fire proceedeth out of their mouth, and devoureth their enemies: and if any man will hurt them, he must in this manner be killed.

⁶ These have power to shut heaven, that it rain not in the days of their prophecy: and have power over waters to turn them to blood, and to smite the earth with all plagues, as often as they will.

⁷ And when they shall have finished their testimony, the beast that ascendeth out of the bottomless pit shall make war against them, and shall overcome them, and kill them.

⁸ And their dead bodies shall lie in the street of the great city, which spiritually is called Sodom and Egypt, where also our Lord was crucified.

⁹ And they of the people and kindreds and tongues and nations shall see their dead bodies three days and an half, and shall not suffer their dead bodies to be put in graves.

¹⁰ And they that dwell upon the earth shall rejoice over them, and make merry, and shall send gifts one to another; because these two prophets tormented them that dwelt on the earth.

[11] And after three days and an half the spirit of life from God entered into them, and they stood upon their feet; and great fear fell upon them which saw them.

[12] And they heard a great voice from heaven saying unto them, Come up hither. And they ascended up to heaven in a cloud; and their enemies beheld them.

[13] And the same hour was there a great earthquake, and the tenth part of the city fell, and in the earthquake were slain of men seven thousand: and the remnant were affrighted, and gave glory to the God of heaven.

[14] The second woe is past; and, behold, the third woe cometh quickly.

[15] And the seventh angel sounded; and there were great voices in heaven, saying, The kingdoms of this world are become the kingdoms of our Lord, and of his Christ; and he shall reign for ever and ever.

[16] And the four and twenty elders, which sat before God on their seats, fell upon their faces, and worshipped God,

[17] Saying, We give thee thanks, O Lord God Almighty, which art, and wast, and art to come; because thou hast taken to thee thy great power, and hast reigned.

[18] And the nations were angry, and thy wrath is come, and the time of the dead, that they should be judged, and that thou shouldest give reward unto thy servants the prophets, and to the saints, and them that fear thy name, small and great; and shouldest destroy them which destroy the earth.

¹⁹ And the temple of God was opened in heaven, and there was seen in his temple the ark of his testament: and there were lightnings, and voices, and thunderings, and an earthquake, and great hail.

12 And there appeared a great wonder in heaven; a woman clothed with the sun, and the moon under her feet, and upon her head a crown of twelve stars:

² And she being with child cried, travailing in birth, and pained to be delivered.

³ And there appeared another wonder in heaven; and behold a great red dragon, having seven heads and ten horns, and seven crowns upon his heads.

⁴ And his tail drew the third part of the stars of heaven, and did cast them to the earth: and the dragon stood before the woman which was ready to be delivered, for to devour her child as soon as it was born.

⁵ And she brought forth a man child, who was to rule all nations with a rod of iron: and her child was caught up unto God, and to his throne.

⁶ And the woman fled into the wilderness, where she hath a place prepared of God, that they should feed her there a thousand two hundred and threescore days.

⁷ And there was war in heaven: Michael and his angels fought against the dragon; and the dragon fought and his angels,

⁸ And prevailed not; neither was their place found any more in heaven.

⁹ And the great dragon was cast out, that old serpent, called the Devil, and Satan, which deceiveth the whole

world: he was cast out into the earth, and his angels were cast out with him.

¹⁰ And I heard a loud voice saying in heaven, Now is come salvation, and strength, and the kingdom of our God, and the power of his Christ: for the accuser of our brethren is cast down, which accused them before our God day and night.

¹¹ And they overcame him by the blood of the Lamb, and by the word of their testimony; and they loved not their lives unto the death.

¹² Therefore rejoice, ye heavens, and ye that dwell in them. Woe to the inhabiters of the earth and of the sea! for the devil is come down unto you, having great wrath, because he knoweth that he hath but a short time.

¹³ And when the dragon saw that he was cast unto the earth, he persecuted the woman which brought forth the man child.

¹⁴ And to the woman were given two wings of a great eagle, that she might fly into the wilderness, into her place, where she is nourished for a time, and times, and half a time, from the face of the serpent.

¹⁵ And the serpent cast out of his mouth water as a flood after the woman, that he might cause her to be carried away of the flood.

¹⁶ And the earth helped the woman, and the earth opened her mouth, and swallowed up the flood which the dragon cast out of his mouth.

¹⁷ And the dragon was wroth with the woman, and went to make war with the remnant of her seed, which keep the commandments of God, and have the testimony of Jesus Christ.

13 And I stood upon the sand of the sea, and saw a beast rise up out of the sea, having seven heads and ten horns, and upon his horns ten crowns, and upon his heads the name of blasphemy.

² And the beast which I saw was like unto a leopard, and his feet were as the feet of a bear, and his mouth as the mouth of a lion: and the dragon gave him his power, and his seat, and great authority.

³ And I saw one of his heads as it were wounded to death; and his deadly wound was healed: and all the world wondered after the beast.

⁴ And they worshipped the dragon which gave power unto the beast: and they worshipped the beast, saying, Who is like unto the beast? who is able to make war with him?

⁵ And there was given unto him a mouth speaking great things and blasphemies; and power was given unto him to continue forty and two months.

⁶ And he opened his mouth in blasphemy against God, to blaspheme his name, and his tabernacle, and them that dwell in heaven.

⁷ And it was given unto him to make war with the saints, and to overcome them: and power was given him over all kindreds, and tongues, and nations.

[8] And all that dwell upon the earth shall worship him, whose names are not written in the book of life of the Lamb slain from the foundation of the world.

[9] If any man have an ear, let him hear.

[10] He that leadeth into captivity shall go into captivity: he that killeth with the sword must be killed with the sword. Here is the patience and the faith of the saints.

[11] And I beheld another beast coming up out of the earth; and he had two horns like a lamb, and he spake as a dragon.

[12] And he exerciseth all the power of the first beast before him, and causeth the earth and them which dwell therein to worship the first beast, whose deadly wound was healed.

[13] And he doeth great wonders, so that he maketh fire come down from heaven on the earth in the sight of men,

[14] And deceiveth them that dwell on the earth by the means of those miracles which he had power to do in the sight of the beast; saying to them that dwell on the earth, that they should make an image to the beast, which had the wound by a sword, and did live.

[15] And he had power to give life unto the image of the beast, that the image of the beast should both speak, and cause that as many as would not worship the image of the beast should be killed.

[16] And he causeth all, both small and great, rich and poor, free and bond, to receive a mark in their right hand, or in their foreheads:

¹⁷ And that no man might buy or sell, save he that had the mark, or the name of the beast, or the number of his name.

¹⁸ Here is wisdom. Let him that hath understanding count the number of the beast: for it is the number of a man; and his number is Six hundred threescore and six.

14 And I looked, and, lo, a Lamb stood on the mount Sion, and with him an hundred forty and four thousand, having his Father's name written in their foreheads.

² And I heard a voice from heaven, as the voice of many waters, and as the voice of a great thunder: and I heard the voice of harpers harping with their harps:

³ And they sung as it were a new song before the throne, and before the four beasts, and the elders: and no man could learn that song but the hundred and forty and four thousand, which were redeemed from the earth.

⁴ These are they which were not defiled with women; for they are virgins. These are they which follow the Lamb whithersoever he goeth. These were redeemed from among men, being the firstfruits unto God and to the Lamb.

⁵ And in their mouth was found no guile: for they are without fault before the throne of God.

⁶ And I saw another angel fly in the midst of heaven, having the everlasting gospel to preach unto them that dwell on the earth, and to every nation, and kindred, and tongue, and people,

⁷ Saying with a loud voice, Fear God, and give glory to him; for the hour of his judgment is come: and worship

him that made heaven, and earth, and the sea, and the fountains of waters.

[8] And there followed another angel, saying, Babylon is fallen, is fallen, that great city, because she made all nations drink of the wine of the wrath of her fornication.

[9] And the third angel followed them, saying with a loud voice, If any man worship the beast and his image, and receive his mark in his forehead, or in his hand,

[10] The same shall drink of the wine of the wrath of God, which is poured out without mixture into the cup of his indignation; and he shall be tormented with fire and brimstone in the presence of the holy angels, and in the presence of the Lamb:

[11] And the smoke of their torment ascendeth up for ever and ever: and they have no rest day nor night, who worship the beast and his image, and whosoever receiveth the mark of his name.

[12] Here is the patience of the saints: here are they that keep the commandments of God, and the faith of Jesus.

[13] And I heard a voice from heaven saying unto me, Write, Blessed are the dead which die in the Lord from henceforth: Yea, saith the Spirit, that they may rest from their labours; and their works do follow them.

[14] And I looked, and behold a white cloud, and upon the cloud one sat like unto the Son of man, having on his head a golden crown, and in his hand a sharp sickle.

[15] And another angel came out of the temple, crying with a loud voice to him that sat on the cloud, Thrust

in thy sickle, and reap: for the time is come for thee to reap; for the harvest of the earth is ripe.

¹⁶ And he that sat on the cloud thrust in his sickle on the earth; and the earth was reaped.

¹⁷ And another angel came out of the temple which is in heaven, he also having a sharp sickle.

¹⁸ And another angel came out from the altar, which had power over fire; and cried with a loud cry to him that had the sharp sickle, saying, Thrust in thy sharp sickle, and gather the clusters of the vine of the earth; for her grapes are fully ripe.

¹⁹ And the angel thrust in his sickle into the earth, and gathered the vine of the earth, and cast it into the great winepress of the wrath of God.

²⁰ And the winepress was trodden without the city, and blood came out of the winepress, even unto the horse bridles, by the space of a thousand and six hundred furlongs.

15 And I saw another sign in heaven, great and marvellous, seven angels having the seven last plagues; for in them is filled up the wrath of God.

² And I saw as it were a sea of glass mingled with fire: and them that had gotten the victory over the beast, and over his image, and over his mark, and over the number of his name, stand on the sea of glass, having the harps of God.

³ And they sing the song of Moses the servant of God, and the song of the Lamb, saying, Great and marvellous

are thy works, Lord God Almighty; just and true are thy ways, thou King of saints.

⁴ Who shall not fear thee, O Lord, and glorify thy name? for thou only art holy: for all nations shall come and worship before thee; for thy judgments are made manifest.

⁵ And after that I looked, and, behold, the temple of the tabernacle of the testimony in heaven was opened:

⁶ And the seven angels came out of the temple, having the seven plagues, clothed in pure and white linen, and having their breasts girded with golden girdles.

⁷ And one of the four beasts gave unto the seven angels seven golden vials full of the wrath of God, who liveth for ever and ever.

⁸ And the temple was filled with smoke from the glory of God, and from his power; and no man was able to enter into the temple, till the seven plagues of the seven angels were fulfilled.

16 And I heard a great voice out of the temple saying to the seven angels, Go your ways, and pour out the vials of the wrath of God upon the earth.

² And the first went, and poured out his vial upon the earth; and there fell a noisome and grievous sore upon the men which had the mark of the beast, and upon them which worshipped his image.

³ And the second angel poured out his vial upon the sea; and it became as the blood of a dead man: and every living soul died in the sea.

⁴ And the third angel poured out his vial upon the rivers and fountains of waters; and they became blood.

⁵ And I heard the angel of the waters say, Thou art righteous, O Lord, which art, and wast, and shalt be, because thou hast judged thus.

⁶ For they have shed the blood of saints and prophets, and thou hast given them blood to drink; for they are worthy.

⁷ And I heard another out of the altar say, Even so, Lord God Almighty, true and righteous are thy judgments.

⁸ And the fourth angel poured out his vial upon the sun; and power was given unto him to scorch men with fire.

⁹ And men were scorched with great heat, and blasphemed the name of God, which hath power over these plagues: and they repented not to give him glory.

¹⁰ And the fifth angel poured out his vial upon the seat of the beast; and his kingdom was full of darkness; and they gnawed their tongues for pain,

¹¹ And blasphemed the God of heaven because of their pains and their sores, and repented not of their deeds.

¹² And the sixth angel poured out his vial upon the great river Euphrates; and the water thereof was dried up, that the way of the kings of the east might be prepared.

¹³ And I saw three unclean spirits like frogs come out of the mouth of the dragon, and out of the mouth of the beast, and out of the mouth of the false prophet.

14 For they are the spirits of devils, working miracles, which go forth unto the kings of the earth and of the whole world, to gather them to the battle of that great day of God Almighty.

15 Behold, I come as a thief. Blessed is he that watcheth, and keepeth his garments, lest he walk naked, and they see his shame.

16 And he gathered them together into a place called in the Hebrew tongue Armageddon.

17 And the seventh angel poured out his vial into the air; and there came a great voice out of the temple of heaven, from the throne, saying, It is done.

18 And there were voices, and thunders, and lightnings; and there was a great earthquake, such as was not since men were upon the earth, so mighty an earthquake, and so great.

19 And the great city was divided into three parts, and the cities of the nations fell: and great Babylon came in remembrance before God, to give unto her the cup of the wine of the fierceness of his wrath.

20 And every island fled away, and the mountains were not found.

21 And there fell upon men a great hail out of heaven, every stone about the weight of a talent: and men blasphemed God because of the plague of the hail; for the plague thereof was exceeding great.

17 And there came one of the seven angels which had the seven vials, and talked with me, saying unto me,

Come hither; I will shew unto thee the judgment of the great whore that sitteth upon many waters:

² With whom the kings of the earth have committed fornication, and the inhabitants of the earth have been made drunk with the wine of her fornication.

³ So he carried me away in the spirit into the wilderness: and I saw a woman sit upon a scarlet coloured beast, full of names of blasphemy, having seven heads and ten horns.

⁴ And the woman was arrayed in purple and scarlet colour, and decked with gold and precious stones and pearls, having a golden cup in her hand full of abominations and filthiness of her fornication:

⁵ And upon her forehead was a name written, Mystery, Babylon The Great, The Mother Of Harlots And Abominations Of The Earth.

⁶ And I saw the woman drunken with the blood of the saints, and with the blood of the martyrs of Jesus: and when I saw her, I wondered with great admiration.

⁷ And the angel said unto me, Wherefore didst thou marvel? I will tell thee the mystery of the woman, and of the beast that carrieth her, which hath the seven heads and ten horns.

⁸ The beast that thou sawest was, and is not; and shall ascend out of the bottomless pit, and go into perdition: and they that dwell on the earth shall wonder, whose names were not written in the book of life from the foundation of the world, when they behold the beast that was, and is not, and yet is.

⁹ And here is the mind which hath wisdom. The seven heads are seven mountains, on which the woman sitteth.

¹⁰ And there are seven kings: five are fallen, and one is, and the other is not yet come; and when he cometh, he must continue a short space.

¹¹ And the beast that was, and is not, even he is the eighth, and is of the seven, and goeth into perdition.

¹² And the ten horns which thou sawest are ten kings, which have received no kingdom as yet; but receive power as kings one hour with the beast.

¹³ These have one mind, and shall give their power and strength unto the beast.

¹⁴ These shall make war with the Lamb, and the Lamb shall overcome them: for he is Lord of lords, and King of kings: and they that are with him are called, and chosen, and faithful.

¹⁵ And he saith unto me, The waters which thou sawest, where the whore sitteth, are peoples, and multitudes, and nations, and tongues.

¹⁶ And the ten horns which thou sawest upon the beast, these shall hate the whore, and shall make her desolate and naked, and shall eat her flesh, and burn her with fire.

¹⁷ For God hath put in their hearts to fulfil his will, and to agree, and give their kingdom unto the beast, until the words of God shall be fulfilled.

¹⁸ And the woman which thou sawest is that great city, which reigneth over the kings of the earth.

18 And after these things I saw another angel come down from heaven, having great power; and the earth was lightened with his glory.

² And he cried mightily with a strong voice, saying, Babylon the great is fallen, is fallen, and is become the habitation of devils, and the hold of every foul spirit, and a cage of every unclean and hateful bird.

³ For all nations have drunk of the wine of the wrath of her fornication, and the kings of the earth have committed fornication with her, and the merchants of the earth are waxed rich through the abundance of her delicacies.

⁴ And I heard another voice from heaven, saying, Come out of her, my people, that ye be not partakers of her sins, and that ye receive not of her plagues.

⁵ For her sins have reached unto heaven, and God hath remembered her iniquities.

⁶ Reward her even as she rewarded you, and double unto her double according to her works: in the cup which she hath filled fill to her double.

⁷ How much she hath glorified herself, and lived deliciously, so much torment and sorrow give her: for she saith in her heart, I sit a queen, and am no widow, and shall see no sorrow.

⁸ Therefore shall her plagues come in one day, death, and mourning, and famine; and she shall be utterly burned with fire: for strong is the Lord God who judgeth her.

⁹ And the kings of the earth, who have committed fornication and lived deliciously with her, shall bewail

her, and lament for her, when they shall see the smoke of her burning,

10 Standing afar off for the fear of her torment, saying, Alas, alas that great city Babylon, that mighty city! for in one hour is thy judgment come.

11 And the merchants of the earth shall weep and mourn over her; for no man buyeth their merchandise any more:

12 The merchandise of gold, and silver, and precious stones, and of pearls, and fine linen, and purple, and silk, and scarlet, and all thyine wood, and all manner vessels of ivory, and all manner vessels of most precious wood, and of brass, and iron, and marble,

13 And cinnamon, and odours, and ointments, and frankincense, and wine, and oil, and fine flour, and wheat, and beasts, and sheep, and horses, and chariots, and slaves, and souls of men.

14 And the fruits that thy soul lusted after are departed from thee, and all things which were dainty and goodly are departed from thee, and thou shalt find them no more at all.

15 The merchants of these things, which were made rich by her, shall stand afar off for the fear of her torment, weeping and wailing,

16 And saying, Alas, alas that great city, that was clothed in fine linen, and purple, and scarlet, and decked with gold, and precious stones, and pearls!

¹⁷ For in one hour so great riches is come to nought. And every shipmaster, and all the company in ships, and sailors, and as many as trade by sea, stood afar off,

¹⁸ And cried when they saw the smoke of her burning, saying, What city is like unto this great city!

¹⁹ And they cast dust on their heads, and cried, weeping and wailing, saying, Alas, alas that great city, wherein were made rich all that had ships in the sea by reason of her costliness! for in one hour is she made desolate.

²⁰ Rejoice over her, thou heaven, and ye holy apostles and prophets; for God hath avenged you on her.

²¹ And a mighty angel took up a stone like a great millstone, and cast it into the sea, saying, Thus with violence shall that great city Babylon be thrown down, and shall be found no more at all.

²² And the voice of harpers, and musicians, and of pipers, and trumpeters, shall be heard no more at all in thee; and no craftsman, of whatsoever craft he be, shall be found any more in thee; and the sound of a millstone shall be heard no more at all in thee;

²³ And the light of a candle shall shine no more at all in thee; and the voice of the bridegroom and of the bride shall be heard no more at all in thee: for thy merchants were the great men of the earth; for by thy sorceries were all nations deceived.

²⁴ And in her was found the blood of prophets, and of saints, and of all that were slain upon the earth.

19 And after these things I heard a great voice of much people in heaven, saying, Alleluia; Salvation, and glory, and honour, and power, unto the Lord our God:

² For true and righteous are his judgments: for he hath judged the great whore, which did corrupt the earth with her fornication, and hath avenged the blood of his servants at her hand.

³ And again they said, Alleluia And her smoke rose up for ever and ever.

⁴ And the four and twenty elders and the four beasts fell down and worshipped God that sat on the throne, saying, Amen; Alleluia.

⁵ And a voice came out of the throne, saying, Praise our God, all ye his servants, and ye that fear him, both small and great.

⁶ And I heard as it were the voice of a great multitude, and as the voice of many waters, and as the voice of mighty thunderings, saying, Alleluia: for the Lord God omnipotent reigneth.

⁷ Let us be glad and rejoice, and give honour to him: for the marriage of the Lamb is come, and his wife hath made herself ready.

⁸ And to her was granted that she should be arrayed in fine linen, clean and white: for the fine linen is the righteousness of saints.

⁹ And he saith unto me, Write, Blessed are they which are called unto the marriage supper of the Lamb. And he saith unto me, These are the true sayings of God.

¹⁰ And I fell at his feet to worship him. And he said unto me, See thou do it not: I am thy fellowservant, and of thy brethren that have the testimony of Jesus: worship God: for the testimony of Jesus is the spirit of prophecy.

¹¹ And I saw heaven opened, and behold a white horse; and he that sat upon him was called Faithful and True, and in righteousness he doth judge and make war.

¹² His eyes were as a flame of fire, and on his head were many crowns; and he had a name written, that no man knew, but he himself.

¹³ And he was clothed with a vesture dipped in blood: and his name is called The Word of God.

¹⁴ And the armies which were in heaven followed him upon white horses, clothed in fine linen, white and clean.

¹⁵ And out of his mouth goeth a sharp sword, that with it he should smite the nations: and he shall rule them with a rod of iron: and he treadeth the winepress of the fierceness and wrath of Almighty God.

¹⁶ And he hath on his vesture and on his thigh a name written, King Of Kings, And Lord Of Lords.

¹⁷ And I saw an angel standing in the sun; and he cried with a loud voice, saying to all the fowls that fly in the midst of heaven, Come and gather yourselves together unto the supper of the great God;

¹⁸ That ye may eat the flesh of kings, and the flesh of captains, and the flesh of mighty men, and the flesh of

horses, and of them that sit on them, and the flesh of all men, both free and bond, both small and great.

¹⁹ And I saw the beast, and the kings of the earth, and their armies, gathered together to make war against him that sat on the horse, and against his army.

²⁰ And the beast was taken, and with him the false prophet that wrought miracles before him, with which he deceived them that had received the mark of the beast, and them that worshipped his image. These both were cast alive into a lake of fire burning with brimstone.

²¹ And the remnant were slain with the sword of him that sat upon the horse, which sword proceeded out of his mouth: and all the fowls were filled with their flesh.

20 And I saw an angel come down from heaven, having the key of the bottomless pit and a great chain in his hand.

² And he laid hold on the dragon, that old serpent, which is the Devil, and Satan, and bound him a thousand years,

³ And cast him into the bottomless pit, and shut him up, and set a seal upon him, that he should deceive the nations no more, till the thousand years should be fulfilled: and after that he must be loosed a little season.

⁴ And I saw thrones, and they sat upon them, and judgment was given unto them: and I saw the souls of them that were beheaded for the witness of Jesus, and for the word of God, and which had not worshipped the beast, neither his image, neither had received his

mark upon their foreheads, or in their hands; and they lived and reigned with Christ a thousand years.

⁵ But the rest of the dead lived not again until the thousand years were finished. This is the first resurrection.

⁶ Blessed and holy is he that hath part in the first resurrection: on such the second death hath no power, but they shall be priests of God and of Christ, and shall reign with him a thousand years.

⁷ And when the thousand years are expired, Satan shall be loosed out of his prison,

⁸ And shall go out to deceive the nations which are in the four quarters of the earth, Gog, and Magog, to gather them together to battle: the number of whom is as the sand of the sea.

⁹ And they went up on the breadth of the earth, and compassed the camp of the saints about, and the beloved city: and fire came down from God out of heaven, and devoured them.

¹⁰ And the devil that deceived them was cast into the lake of fire and brimstone, where the beast and the false prophet are, and shall be tormented day and night for ever and ever.

¹¹ And I saw a great white throne, and him that sat on it, from whose face the earth and the heaven fled away; and there was found no place for them.

¹² And I saw the dead, small and great, stand before God; and the books were opened: and another book was opened, which is the book of life: and the dead

were judged out of those things which were written in the books, according to their works.

¹³ And the sea gave up the dead which were in it; and death and hell delivered up the dead which were in them: and they were judged every man according to their works.

¹⁴ And death and hell were cast into the lake of fire. This is the second death.

¹⁵ And whosoever was not found written in the book of life was cast into the lake of fire.

21 And I saw a new heaven and a new earth: for the first heaven and the first earth were passed away; and there was no more sea.

² And I John saw the holy city, new Jerusalem, coming down from God out of heaven, prepared as a bride adorned for her husband.

³ And I heard a great voice out of heaven saying, Behold, the tabernacle of God is with men, and he will dwell with them, and they shall be his people, and God himself shall be with them, and be their God.

⁴ And God shall wipe away all tears from their eyes; and there shall be no more death, neither sorrow, nor crying, neither shall there be any more pain: for the former things are passed away.

⁵ And he that sat upon the throne said, Behold, I make all things new. And he said unto me, Write: for these words are true and faithful.

⁶ And he said unto me, It is done. I am Alpha and Omega, the beginning and the end. I will give unto

him that is athirst of the fountain of the water of life freely.

⁷ He that overcometh shall inherit all things; and I will be his God, and he shall be my son.

⁸ But the fearful, and unbelieving, and the abominable, and murderers, and whoremongers, and sorcerers, and idolaters, and all liars, shall have their part in the lake which burneth with fire and brimstone: which is the second death.

⁹ And there came unto me one of the seven angels which had the seven vials full of the seven last plagues, and talked with me, saying, Come hither, I will shew thee the bride, the Lamb's wife.

¹⁰ And he carried me away in the spirit to a great and high mountain, and shewed me that great city, the holy Jerusalem, descending out of heaven from God,

¹¹ Having the glory of God: and her light was like unto a stone most precious, even like a jasper stone, clear as crystal;

¹² And had a wall great and high, and had twelve gates, and at the gates twelve angels, and names written thereon, which are the names of the twelve tribes of the children of Israel:

¹³ On the east three gates; on the north three gates; on the south three gates; and on the west three gates.

¹⁴ And the wall of the city had twelve foundations, and in them the names of the twelve apostles of the Lamb.

¹⁵ And he that talked with me had a golden reed to measure the city, and the gates thereof, and the wall thereof.

¹⁶ And the city lieth foursquare, and the length is as large as the breadth: and he measured the city with the reed, twelve

thousand furlongs. The length and the breadth and the height of it are equal.

¹⁷ And he measured the wall thereof, an hundred and forty and four cubits, according to the measure of a man, that is, of the angel.

¹⁸ And the building of the wall of it was of jasper: and the city was pure gold, like unto clear glass.

¹⁹ And the foundations of the wall of the city were garnished with all manner of precious stones. The first foundation was jasper; the second, sapphire; the third, a chalcedony; the fourth, an emerald;

²⁰ The fifth, sardonyx; the sixth, sardius; the seventh, chrysolyte; the eighth, beryl; the ninth, a topaz; the tenth, a chrysoprasus; the eleventh, a jacinth; the twelfth, an amethyst.

²¹ And the twelve gates were twelve pearls: every several gate was of one pearl: and the street of the city was pure gold, as it were transparent glass.

²² And I saw no temple therein: for the Lord God Almighty and the Lamb are the temple of it.

²³ And the city had no need of the sun, neither of the moon, to shine in it: for the glory of God did lighten it, and the Lamb is the light thereof.

²⁴ And the nations of them which are saved shall walk in the light of it: and the kings of the earth do bring their glory and honour into it.

²⁵ And the gates of it shall not be shut at all by day: for there shall be no night there.

²⁶ And they shall bring the glory and honour of the nations into it.

²⁷ And there shall in no wise enter into it any thing that defileth, neither whatsoever worketh abomination, or maketh a lie: but they which are written in the Lamb's book of life.

22 And he shewed me a pure river of water of life, clear as crystal, proceeding out of the throne of God and of the Lamb.

² In the midst of the street of it, and on either side of the river, was there the tree of life, which bare twelve manner of fruits, and yielded her fruit every month: and the leaves of the tree were for the healing of the nations.

³ And there shall be no more curse: but the throne of God and of the Lamb shall be in it; and his servants shall serve him:

⁴ And they shall see his face; and his name shall be in their foreheads.

⁵ And there shall be no night there; and they need no candle, neither light of the sun; for the Lord God giveth them light: and they shall reign for ever and ever.

⁶ And he said unto me, These sayings are faithful and true: and the Lord God of the holy prophets sent his

angel to shew unto his servants the things which must shortly be done.

7 Behold, I come quickly: blessed is he that keepeth the sayings of the prophecy of this book.

8 And I John saw these things, and heard them. And when I had heard and seen, I fell down to worship before the feet of the angel which shewed me these things.

9 Then saith he unto me, See thou do it not: for I am thy fellowservant, and of thy brethren the prophets, and of them which keep the sayings of this book: worship God.

10 And he saith unto me, Seal not the sayings of the prophecy of this book: for the time is at hand.

11 He that is unjust, let him be unjust still: and he which is filthy, let him be filthy still: and he that is righteous, let him be righteous still: and he that is holy, let him be holy still.

12 And, behold, I come quickly; and my reward is with me, to give every man according as his work shall be.

13 I am Alpha and Omega, the beginning and the end, the first and the last.

14 Blessed are they that do his commandments, that they may have right to the tree of life, and may enter in through the gates into the city.

15 For without are dogs, and sorcerers, and whoremongers, and murderers, and idolaters, and whosoever loveth and maketh a lie.

16 I Jesus have sent mine angel to testify unto you these things in the churches. I am the root and the offspring of David, and the bright and morning star.

17 And the Spirit and the bride say, Come. And let him that heareth say, Come. And let him that is athirst come. And whosoever will, let him take the water of life freely.

18 For I testify unto every man that heareth the words of the prophecy of this book, If any man shall add unto these things, God shall add unto him the plagues that are written in this book:

19 And if any man shall take away from the words of the book of this prophecy, God shall take away his part out of the book of life, and out of the holy city, and from the things which are written in this book.

20 He which testifieth these things saith, Surely I come quickly. Amen. Even so, come, Lord Jesus.

21 The grace of our Lord Jesus Christ be with you all. Amen.

IMPORTANT NOTES

The Book of Revelation has twists, and turns that require close attention, and these are the visions which are"

The Vision of the Seven Churches (Rev. 1:9–3:22)

The Vision of the Seven Seals (Rev. 4:1–8:1)

The Vision of the Seven Trumpets (Rev. 8:2–11:19)

The Vision of the Seven Mystic 3 Figures (Rev. 12:1–14:20)

The Vision of the Seven Vials (Rev. 15:1–16:21)

The Vision of the Great Whore (Rev. 17:1–20:15)

The Vision of the Bride (Rev. 21:1–22:7)

In conclusion, I would say that the Book of Revelation is a guide and a beacon for those willing to die for what they believed

THE REVELATION
Prophecy Chart

The BOOK of REVELATION			
INTRODUCTION		Ch. 1	THE CHURCH AGE
EPHESUS *The Loveless Church*		Chapters 2 · 3	
SMYRNA *The Suffering Church*			
PERGAMOS *The Church of Satan's City*			
THYATIRA *The Adulterous Church*			
SARDIS *The Dead Church*			
PHILADELPHIA *The Faithful Church*			
LAODICEA *The Disgusting Church*			

BEGINNING OF THE CHURCH AGE
- Death of Christ
- Burial of Christ
- Resurrection of Christ
- Descent of the Holy Spirit

LETTERS *to the* SEVEN CHURCHES

Judgment Seat of Christ

RAPTURE—*Jesus Comes for the Church*

1. White Horse *Conquering Power*			THE TRIBULATION PERIOD
2. Red Horse *War and Bloodshed*		Chapters 6:1 - 8:6	
3. Black Horse *Famine*			
4. Pale Horse *Pestilence and Death*			
5. Souls Under the Altar *Martyrs*			
6. Whole World Trembles *Physical Changes*			
Interval *144,000 Sealed*			
7. Silence—Golden Censer			

SEVEN SEALS *the*

101

1. Hail and Fire Mixed With Blood		
2. A Mountain Thrown Into the Sea		
3. The Star Wormwood		
4. A Third of the Sun, Moon, and Stars Struck	*the* SEVEN TRUMPETS	Chapters 8:7 - 11:19
5. The Plague of Locusts		
6. Release of the Four Angels		
The Angel and the Little Book		
The Two Witnesses		
7. Woe on Earth, Worship in Heaven		

Hell on Earth (beside trumpets 5 & 6)

WAR IN HEAVEN		
SATAN'S FALL FROM HEAVEN	THE COUNTERFEIT TRINITY	Chapters 12 - 14
THE BEAST FROM THE SEA		
THE BEAST FROM THE EARTH		
THE LAMB AND THE 144,000		
200 MILES OF BLOODSHED		

- The Dragon (Anti-God)
- The Beast (Anti-Christ)
- The False Prophet (Anti-Spirit)

1. Ugly and Painful Sores		
2. Sea Turns to Blood		
3. Rivers and Streams of Water Become Blood	*the* SEVEN BOWLS	Chapters 15 - 16
4. Sun Scorches People With Fire		
5. Darkness		
6. Euphrates River Dries Up		
7. Tremendous Earthquake—Armageddon		

The Earth's Worst Days

END OF FALSE RELIGION		Chs. 17 - 19
COLLAPSE OF THE WORLD MARKET		
SECOND COMING—*Jesus Comes With the Church*		*Marriage Supper of the Lamb*

THE TRIBULATION PERIOD

continued on next page...

MILLENNIUM		
Chapter 2011 - 6	Chapter 2017 - 14	Chapters 21 - 22

the
1,000-YEAR REIGN
of
JESUS CHRIST
and All the Saints

A period of peace and righteousness will last for a millennium.

the
GREAT WHITE THRONE JUDGMENT

THE LAKE OF FIRE
Satan, demons, fallen angels, and unrepented sinners are eternally separated from God.

the
NEW HEAVEN *and* **NEW EARTH**

The BOOK *of* REVELATION

Scripture	Summary	Date
Revelation 6-11	The events leading up to the destruction of Jerusalem in 70 AD.	Up to 70 AD
Revelation 12	Events of the birth of the church and the church's flight to Pella shown in signs, including Christ's birth.	66 AD
Revelation 13	The Two Beasts. Foresees Domitian's Reign as the Beast, "Nero back for the pit", and the Imperial Cult as the False Prophet.	Ended in Sept. 96 AD
Revelation 14:1-5	First-fruits church. The original generation of believers has gone on to be with the Lord. The "fruit that remains" is the church through the ages.	Circa 100 AD
Revelation 14:6-13	The three angels. The Gospel will now spread throughout the world, Babylon will fall, and those who submit to Emperor worship while it still remains will receive the same fate as it.	...
Revelation 14:14-20	The two harvests, and the WinePress of His Wrath. Seen in the Siege of Betar in the Second Jewish Revolt, during which over 500,000 Jews were killed in the city of Betar, just outside of Jerusalem in 135 AD.	132–135 AD
Revelation 15-16	The Seven Bowls of Wrath. Seen as the final wrath against Babylon, which is Rome. The purpose was the breakdown of the empire, and was witnessed in the "Crisis of the Third Century", resulting in the empire being broken up into three warring factions, and the loss of the Principate.	250–271 AD

Revelation 17-19	The Fall of Babylon, the Great Harlot. Seen as Rome, the spiritual power of Rome was broken through the conversion of its emperor to Christianity Constantine's conversion led to the legalization of Christianity and the end of the outward persecution of the church.	Circa 300 AD
Revelation 20:1-6	The Millennium. Foxxe's book of martyr's records no martyrs for 1000 years following the Edict of Milan in 313 AD. Literally, the murderer himself, but not all demons, were bound and locked into the pit until the thousand years were up.	Circa 313 AD
Revelation 20:7-10	Persecution begins again in the church against John Wycliffe. This was followed by the martyrdom of John Huss in 1415. By the year of 1522, when Martin Luther posted his 95 theses, the "renaissance", or "rebirth of the dragon from the pit", was in full swing, with the rebellion against the church, the separation of "knowledge, science, and understanding" from the Word of God, and the promotion of secularization. Since this time, the working of the dragon has been to subvert the Word of God with things such as Evolution and Humanism, and ultimately to deceive the nations and bring them again to ultimately attack the church. In the period of this "short time" is the evidence, over the few centuries, of the coercion of the nations towards this end, and as Israel is now a nation and sin and morality continue to degenerate, it is only increasing.	1371–1522 Ongoing Will end with the Gog Magog war, and the judgment of the dragon. This period ends, according to Ezekiel 39:28-29 with the salvation of all Israel, after much trial.
Revelation 20:11-15	The Second Coming, the appearing of the Lord in the Great White Throne Judgment seat. Corresponds to Matthew 24:29-31.	"Day and Hour Unknown"

REFERENCE

Hole Bible

Bert Hovestadt and William Marrion Branham - Book of Revelation, Explained: Poem

Larry R. Helyer, Richard Wagner, Richard Wagner - The Book of Revelation for Dummies

Rabbi Kirt A. Schneider - The Book of Revelation Decoded Revised Edition: Your Guide to Understanding the End Times Through the Eyes of the Hebrew Prophets Paperback – January 7, 2025

Kenneth L. Barker - The Expositor's Bible Commentary - Abridged Edition: Two-Volume Set Hardcover – Abridged, May 10, 2004

www.ingramcontent.com/pod-product-compliance
Lightning Source LLC
Chambersburg PA
CBHW051218120626
46547CB00013B/1403